Sewing HOPE

JOSEPH KONY TORE THESE GIRLS' LIVES APART.
CAN SHE STITCH THEM BACK TOGETHER?

D1562910

REGGIE WHITTEN
and NANCY HENDERSON

dustjacket

ISBN: 978-0-692-44948-6

Dust Jacket Press
PO Box 721243
Oklahoma City, OK 73172

www.DustJacket.com
Info@DustJacket.com

Cover Title & Interior Design: DustJacket

Printed in United States of America

DEDICATION

To Sister Rosemary Nyirumbe
and others who bring hope and healing to a violent world

MAPS OF UGANDA

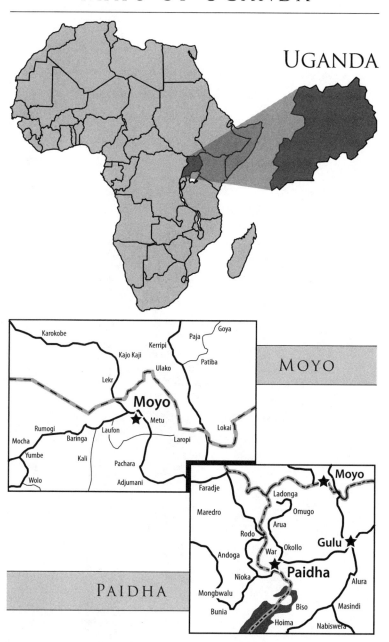

UGANDA

MOYO

Karokobe
Kajo Kaji
Kerripi
Paja
Goya
Ulako
Patiba
Lekr
Moyo
Metu
Lokai
Rumogi
Laufon
Laropi
Mocha
Baringa
Yumbe
Kali
Pachara
Wolo
Adjumani

Faradje
Ladonga
Moyo
Maredro
Omugo
Arua
Rodo
Gulu
Andoga
Okollo
War
Paidha
Nioka
Alura
Mongbwalu
Biso
Masindi
Bunia
Hoima
Nabiswera

PAIDHA

CONTENTS

INTRODUCTION

She held the small purse in her aching hands and stared at it in the moonlight. What an unusual thing, she thought, this unlikely blend of silver pop tabs sewn together with jet-black thread and a label inside that read "Handmade by St. Monica's Girls School, Gulu, Uganda." Considered by most to be mere trash, of no value and ready for the garbage heap, pop tabs now offered a lifeline for many in her community and a significant source of income for her schools, much-needed food and clean water.

Suddenly, it occurred to her how similar these abandoned, seemingly insignificant objects were to the young girls she had taken under her wing. Once viewed as innocent and beautiful, these children were now considered by most of the world to be worthless, discarded, a mere afterthought in the shadow of a terrible war. Kidnapped, stolen from their parents at a tender age and forced to serve as sex slaves, "wives" and soldiers in a war they didn't create, they were often shunned by their own communities and called disparaging names like "returnees" or "school dropouts" despite the fact that they had been abducted, violently and against their will. These innocent victims were just like the pop tabs: rubble to be tossed onto the scrap heap of history and forgotten.

Sister Rosemary Nyirumbe placed the little purse on a nearby table, rubbed her hands and walked across the dirt courtyard to her school. This was one of her favorite times of the day, when the students and their children were asleep and the place was completely silent. Looking around, with these angels safe in their beds, she knew all the hard work had been worth it and that, if given a choice, she would do it all over again.

The persistent pain in her thumbs was caused by *stenosing tenosynovitis*, or trigger thumb, an inflammatory condition generally caused by overuse. She needed surgery, but here in Gulu, in northern Uganda, she had virtually no access to medical treatment, even for emergencies. Living with pain was nothing new for Sister Rosemary and her girls. There was no doctor for the sick, no medicine for the weak and no place to go for help. They were truly on their own, and had been for decades.

Sewing pop tab purses each day made the pain almost unbearable. But sew she did, until her hands bled. Then she sewed some more, until the aluminum tabs, cloth lining and stitches were one. What was once rubble was now a beautiful purse, a unique, functional work of art and a source of pride for the students who learned to make them under the caring tutelage of a Catholic nun who loved the girls as if they were her own.

Back in her bed, as she gazed out the window at the moon high in the sky, it occurred to Sister Rosemary that her life, too, was a lot like the pop tabs. She owned nothing—this was her choice, having taken a vow of poverty—even after a long life of hard work. She had seen many things, some wonderful and many terrible, but she and the young ladies at her school were now bound together, not with thread, but with a pure and selfless love.

Resting her hands, she closed her eyes and sighed deeply. She had lived in grave danger, surviving the violent dictatorship of former Ugandan president Idi Amin and the senseless war led by terrorist Joseph Kony and the Lord's Resistance Army. She had seen enough evil for many lifetimes and knew she was fortunate to have not been killed by the LRA thugs she had encountered over the years.

More recently, she had come to know a different type of army, a gentle army of people with love in their hearts, who had been miraculously drawn here to give hope to her girls. This new group—volunteer professionals who had traveled thousands of miles from the United States—were determined to help weave the lives of her girls, like pop tab purses, into something beautiful. In the years since the war had ended, travelers had been afraid to come to northern Uganda even though Kony was believed to be long gone. But tonight was different. A ragtag group of volunteers from a place far away was here to help, to spread hope. Perhaps by their coming, the world would remember the atrocities committed by Kony and his thugs and make sure they were never, ever repeated.

Finally at peace, Sister Rosemary set off to bed. Tomorrow, she must instruct her girls on more purse making and make sure her American guests were comfortable. She usually didn't sleep well, and only for a few hours at a time. But tonight she just might be able to relax, because she had hope—hope that these girls, who had been through a hell few could imagine, would lead meaningful lives and heal from the past.

If a small mound of trash can be turned into a beautiful purse, if a little girl who has been kidnapped, raped and stripped of her dignity, can be transformed into a proud and productive citizen, then anything is possible, Sister Rosemary knew. Indeed, anything is possible, if only one has hope, and a dream.

I will not stop dreaming, she thought as she drifted off to sleep.

Sister Rosemary woke with a start, her hands stiff and sore. The same nightmare, the same story *Sharon had told her three years ago, had interrupted her slumber on other nights too.

At twenty, Sharon wore her hair short, shaved close to the head like a boy's, as if by doing so she could somehow deny her own gender. She tended to keep to herself, preferring to be alone rather than mingle with the other girls, and frequently stared at the ground, her chin angled downward, pressed close to her throat. When she bent her head in the sunlight, the disfiguring outline of a burn scar glistened just beneath her dark, cropped hair. The inside of one forearm, from the wrist to the crook of her elbow, bore permanent stripes from a different kind of burn. She never smiled.

Sharon had been abducted by Kony's rebel soldiers and had managed to escape in 2005. After five years of struggling to make it on her own, she had come to St. Monica's to live and learn job skills with other girls who had been held captive in the bush. It took Sharon another year to muster the courage to share her story with Sister Rosemary.

After tailoring class one afternoon, the compassionate nun felt it was time to broach the subject. "Do you want to tell me what happened when you were living in the bush?" she gently asked, prepared to drop the subject if Sharon didn't want to talk.

"I can't," the girl said, shaking her head. "You would never forgive me."

"Forgive you? Why would you need my forgiveness?"

Sharon took a deep breath. Then, in a rare moment since the insurgents had snatched the thirteen-year-old from her parents' home in the middle of the night, she allowed the words to escape from her lips.

"Because," she whispered, tears pooling in her black eyes, "they made me kill my own sister."

---

*The names of the former abductees in this book have been changed to protect them from harm.

PART ONE

CHAPTER ONE

OF COFFEE AND CATERPILLARS

2007 CNN Hero

The town of Paidha lies in the West Nile sub-region of northern Uganda, a land that, like much of the country, is at once lushly fertile and drenched in poverty.

Sidled against the eastern edge of the Democratic Republic of Congo—so close, in fact, that Paidha residents sometimes spot their Congo neighbors beyond the forested border—the busy crossing town is a rich source of aromatic Arabica coffee beans, a milder species than the more bitter kind grown commercially in southern Uganda. Disease-resistant bananas thrive in the tropical climate, as do thickets of hot-pink hibiscus and other flowering shrubs, while the busy central town market brims with baskets of fresh vegetables, live chickens, and mugs of *kwete*, a gentle, traditional brew of fermented maize, malt and yeast.

The filth of privation is, however, undeniable. Few cars travel the dirt streets, and owning a bicycle, though more common, is still considered a luxury. A single community stream, shared with the village goats and cows, supplies water for cooking, bathing and drinking, which accounts for widespread eye infections, parasitic infestations and other diseases among infants and adults. Except for a few sparse wells, there are no sources of clean drinking water, and many families are so poor that they struggle to feed their children a few spoonfuls of boiled millet or beans each day.

For those who grew up in Paidha, life before the rule of military dictator Idi Amin in the early 1970s and, two decades later, Joseph Kony and his brutal Lord's Resistance Army, was much simpler, safer, a happier place. Back then, before the destructive economic policies and outright terrorism brought even more financial instability to Uganda, it was easier to overlook the poverty and appreciate every blessing, no matter how small.

For Rosemary Nyirumbe, who was born here in 1956, Paidha was the type of town that instills a longing in the heart when one is gone.

Martino Orwodhi was just a boy, the oldest son in his family, when a group of Frenchmen from the Congo approached his uncles, looking for young men to train in the art of carpentry.

"These people are lying; there is no school," the uncles said with suspicion. "They are coming to take our children, to sell them into slavery, and we will never see them again."

To appease the French carpenters, they conspired, "Let us give them this boy who is not ours, but our sister's."

Their fear turned out to be Martino's good fortune. The French artisans taught him well, even giving him a set of tools with which to start his own workshop, and a few years later the quiet young man emerged as one of the Congo's first skilled carpenters, quickly gaining a reputation as the best in town, carving furniture from mahogany and preparing his own varnish from the sap of wild trees. He married a soft-spoken woman named Sabina Otiti, and the couple had five children in Congo—the second baby, Emelio, did not survive—and three more after moving from the small town of Mahagi to Paidha to expose their offspring to a proper Ugandan education. Raising the children in Uganda, Martino's native country, would force them to learn English, the common, official language in a nation with dozens of Swahili dialects separating one tribe from another and blocking communication among the various villages. Situated within Paidha and home to fewer than 500 people, Martino's village would come to be called Jopandika, named for his grandfather.

Sabina was an active member of the Democratic Party, Uganda's moderate conservative political group, and often led other women in peaceful demonstrations of solidarity on behalf of the High Church of the Roman Catholic faith, which, according to Democratic supporters, was being threatened by the newer Ugandan People's Congress comprised mainly of Anglicans. Martino silently tolerated his wife's involvement in such matters and avoided politics altogether, preferring to concentrate on his woodworking and, in the evening, the family garden.

After a full day of crafting tables and chairs to sell at the weekend market, and sometimes again in the early morning before he went to his workshop, he would head to the fields and join his wife to dig the soil, plant seedlings and tend the long rows of maize and groundnuts. Unlike many proud African men, he saw no embarrassment in "woman's work"—gathering bananas, peeling them and boiling the fruit for a meal, or plucking ripe coffee beans from the trees, grinding the pits and preparing a robust beverage for breakfast.

Each morning, Martino invited his children to line up for a cup of his bitter coffee, boiled in a pot and served with no sugar. Young Rosemary hated the strong taste at first, but as the years passed, she developed a love for the drink and refused the milder afternoon tea.

Martino made little effort to hide the fact that he favored his daughters Martha, Catherine, Perpetua and Rosemary over his sons Valerio, Thomas, Luigi and Santos. One of nine brothers in a family with no sisters, Martino felt especially honored when his firstborn was a girl, adding a feminine branch to the family tree. As is customary in Uganda, each child bore a different surname, often written or spoken before the first name.

Still not satisfied with the number of girls he fathered, to Rosemary, the youngest, he teasingly gave the last name *Nyirumbe*, which translates to "girls (*nyir*) are not there (*umbe*)" in the family's tribal dialect, Alur. Martino's nickname for his favorite daughter—Rosemary Nyaraliga, his own mother's name—was so commonly used in the family home that, when asked to state her name on the first day of pre-school, the little girl replied without hesitation, "Rosemary Nyaraliga."

"That doesn't sound right," scolded the teacher, who proceeded to call on Martha, a teacher at the same school, to solve the puzzle.

"Can you explain if this is the true name of this child?" the teacher asked Rosemary's older sister. "She says it's Nyaraliga but we have no record of this."

"No, she is called Rosemary Nyirumbe," Martha replied, not knowing whether to be irritated or amused.

Education was a high priority for Martino and Sabina, who treated their boys and girls equally in a country where females were often relegated to subservient roles. Both daughters and sons were expected to toil in the garden and learn basic skills in Martino's workshop, where he taught them how to wield a hammer and hold the mahogany planks while he used a plane to smooth the rough edges. Rosemary often ground flour with her little brother Santos, rubbing it between two stones until thick calluses formed on the heels of her hands.

Sabina, in particular, insisted that all eight of her children attend school. To help pay the tuition, she brewed *nguli*, a high-alcohol-content beer distilled from yeast and cassava, a yam-like root, and walked long distances to sell it. "I'll do anything to make sure you go to school," she told Catherine one day. "If it means I have to walk naked because I have no money for clothes, I will send you to school."

Martino's brothers were of a different mind. "Why are you educating those girls?" they scoffed. "You are sending them for nothing. Girls are meant to be married off and you are wasting their dowry."

Each time Martino was tempted to agree with them, his wife convinced him otherwise.

Despite the family's shortage of money—it was not uncommon for the children to go to bed hungry when there was no food in the house, then eat only sweet bananas for breakfast, a morning habit she would continue for the rest of her life—Rosemary felt happy and loved. When she cried for attention, her father lifted her in his arms and carried her on his back, bouncing her up and down. Combing the tangles from her daughter's long hair, her mother often crooned, "Rosemary, you are the most beautiful baby in the world." Her siblings seemed to harbor no resentment toward their little sister and pampered her too. Not wanting to leave her behind, her parents took her with them when they visited friends, even for a few days, and her sisters sewed clothes for her from pieces of their own smocks. When they grew up and moved away, they always returned with new dresses for Rosemary, as if they were practicing the styles they would someday make for their own children. Even on nights the family was forced to go without dinner, Rosemary slept well, secure in the knowledge that morning would come all the same, and with it a meal.

Sweet-tempered, playful and quick to learn, Rosemary was by no means a squeamish little girl sheltered from real life. Charming her brothers into letting her play football with them, she developed a knack for the game and would often sprint past them on the field. She also became quite adept at climbing the trees in the family's yard. One day while her parents were digging in the garden, she shimmied up the branches of a huge mango, up, up, up, until she suddenly lost her footing and fell to the ground. She would forever carry the scar from the gash in her lower abdomen.

The mango tree, however, carried far more significance than that of a childhood mishap. Customarily, when a Ugandan woman is in labor, she will go outside and wait, then seek shelter when it is time to give birth. Rosemary emerged from her mother's womb in a tiny hut a few paces from the tree, her umbilical cord soon buried near its roots as a symbol of her lifelong connection to the place where she was born.

Strong and athletic, Rosemary showed no fear of getting hurt or trying new things. The sight of one creature, however, absolutely terrified her. If, while weeding the crops or digging potatoes, she encountered a large, fuzzy caterpillar, she would scream, flail about as if she had seen a poisonous viper, and run away as fast as she could. Sabina knew she had to do something. "Okay, we are not taking you to the garden any more because you are disrupting the work of the other children. What else do you think you can do if you don't go to the garden with us?"

"I think I can cook," Rosemary replied. "I can look after the house. When all of you come back, you will find the food ready." This role suited Rosemary well, and she became quite proficient at cooking and keeping a tidy home, which was made up of a cluster of small, round mud houses with thatched roofs and dirt floors. Twice a month, the children would collect cow dung to smear on the walls to keep dust away and maintain the huts.

A single, covered outdoor latrine served not only the family, but sometimes the entire village. Luckily, Rosemary's father was a man of good hygiene. Meticulous about the dugout, he taught his offspring the proper way to care for it.

"This is something you must know," Martino told them. "Whenever someone comes to visit, he will be able to tell if you are a clean person by the way you keep your latrine. So your latrine must always be clean, with no smell."

In keeping with Ugandan customs, at night the girls slept in one house, the boys in another, the parents in a third. The older children served as mentors to their younger siblings, teaching appropriate habits, traditions and behaviors expected of those entering into maturity. Sometimes at the end of the workday, the family shared their evening meal at the table. Other times the boys ate with their father, the girls with their mother. Because Rosemary chewed her food slowly, and took very little for herself, Sabina sat next to her youngest daughter so the brothers wouldn't snatch her portion.

When she was quite small, Rosemary began absorbing the English words her older siblings were learning, sometimes poring over their books at night in an effort to translate sentences from her native Alur. By the time she started school, she was already proficient in English and reading, and she quickly rose to the top of her class.

To the delight of his children, before bedtime Martino often settled into a corner to strum his *adungu*, a small arched harp with nine strings twisted from plant fibers. Balancing the wooden base between his knees, he would pluck the varying lengths of string and begin to sing, with or without an audience. In later years, Rosemary would come to realize that Martino's music served another purpose: to protect his beloved daughters by enticing them to stay at home and listen rather than venture out after dark.

A wonderful storyteller, Rosemary's mother had her own ways of keeping her children out of trouble. On moonlit nights, the family gathered around an outdoor fire and listened to Sabina recount the legend of how the *Luo* tribes came to be:

Once upon a time, there were two brothers, Gipir and Labongo, the great-grandchildren of Luo, who sprang from the ground with no human parents, the world's first man. Born with feathers in his hair and bells circling his wrists and ankles, Labongo loved to dance and was said to be the offspring of a woman named Nyilak and the devil himself.

One day, when they were grown, a conflict arose between Labongo and Gipir when one of their children swallowed a magic bead belonging to the other. "I want my bead back," insisted the sibling from whom it had been "stolen." "I will get it for you," replied his brother, confident the bauble would soon show up in the baby's feces. But when the baby relieved itself, the bead was nowhere in sight. Furious, the wronged sibling cut the infant in half and retrieved the bead from its lifeless body.

According to Sabina's version of the story, Gipir was called Nyipir, and Labongo took on the name of Nyabongo. The brothers continued to co-exist, each silently seething in hate against the other. Years later, Gipir borrowed his sibling's spear to go hunting. Gipir struck an elephant but did not kill it, and the animal ran with the weapon still in its side. "I lost your spear," Gipir sheepishly told Labongo when he came back. "The elephant is now far away."

Seizing an opportunity for revenge, Labongo replied, "I want nothing but my spear. Bring it back to me—now."

Gipir searched for the elephant but it was long gone, and once again he returned empty-handed. Driving an enormous ax into the ground and splitting the earth into a deep chasm, Labongo declared, "From this day, we must turn our backs on each other and never speak again."

Gipir moved west toward Congo and begat a long line of descendants, including the Alur, while Labongo moved east of the Nile and became the forefather of the present-day Acholi. From then on, relationships between the various Luo tribes of northern Uganda were complicated, strained, and filled with conflict.

"My children, you must always forgive and never, ever do anything out of revenge," Sabina said each time she reached the end of the story. Rosemary took the moral to heart and, in future years, would recall the fate of the brothers who could not forgive.

When Rosemary was five years old, her parents sent her to live with her oldest sister Martha. Martha was the first girl in the village to finish her studies and the first to have a modern wedding. She was also the first girl in her family who dreamed of becoming a nun. "No Martha, that is out of the question," her parents argued despite their strong religious convictions. "You must earn a proper living and help pay the school fees for your younger brothers and sisters. Our hopes are in you."

So Martha became a teacher and helped finance the education of her siblings, who were not much younger than herself. Valerio managed to get by in his studies, but Catherine, the third-born, won many scholarships and grew up to become a political leader in the community.

"Giving" a child to an older sibling is not a Ugandan tradition, but when Martha was newly married, Martino and

Sabina felt she would be lonely without the company of her brothers and sisters, so they packed most of Rosemary's things and took the little girl to Martha's new house, perhaps in part to make up for denying the older sister's wish to join the convent. Martha treated Rosemary as if she were her firstborn—the two even bore a striking physical resemblance—and for a time, gossiping villagers accused Martha of giving birth to a child out of wedlock. After a while, even Rosemary began to think of Martha as her real mother.

Indeed, Martha loved Rosemary like a daughter and so did her husband Geraldo, who was also a teacher. Life was more modern, more physically comfortable, at Martha's home, where Rosemary received her own little mattress and housekeepers bathed her each day. Her parents visited often, and she frequently biked the half-mile to their house down a narrow dirt road. She had taught herself to ride at a very young age, sneaking her father's bicycle out after dark so she could practice and pedal as well as her brothers. Her mother had acquired a bike after becoming a teacher but had never ridden it, so Rosemary used it to get from the school to Martha's house and back even though it was much too large for her.

On weekends, Martha and Geraldo took the child with them to watch films in the town center. One time, she even accompanied Martha to Kampala, the capital city of Uganda, where she stayed in a big hotel for a week and slept on a baby cot near her caretaker. Ambitious and visionary, Martha was a role model for many women in the village, representing a level of education, sophistication and understanding of the world Rosemary had not encountered while living in her father's house.

She quickly adapted to her new life, never homesick for what she had left behind. It took a while, however, for her to get used to sleeping alone in a room with no siblings.

"I need the light to be on all night," Rosemary told her sister. "Someone will come and get me if you don't leave the light on."

"No, Rosemary, our house is right by the roadside," Martha assured her. "If we leave the light on, somebody might see you. This way you are totally safe."

About a year after Rosemary went to live with her sister, Martha gave birth to the first of eight children. Rosemary had no idea that, by babysitting her nieces and nephews, she was honing her maternal instincts and preparing to care for the many orphans she would nurture throughout her career. She adored Martha's children, so much so that rather than resenting her older sister for giving her so much responsibility, she looked forward to biking from school each day during class break to check on the little ones. She fed them, changed their diapers and affectionately carried them on her back, just as her father had carried *her*.

Rosemary was also expected to keep Martha's house impeccably clean and complete every task with precision, no matter how small. At dinner, the elder sister checked each water flask brought to the table; if one showed a spot or a trace of grime, Rosemary would be asked to take it back to the kitchen and give it a thorough cleaning. And unlike many

Paidha residents, Martha insisted the floors be scrubbed with detergent, not pure water.

"If you are going to put milk in a bottle, make sure you boil the bottle first," Martha instructed. "And if you're boiling cows' milk, heat it to a boil, add a little bit of water, then let it boil again. Then cool it, put it in a clean bottle and give it to the child. It must be very sterilized."

Rosemary adhered to her sister's rules, but she was far from perfect. Stubborn and willful, she often dirtied her clothes as soon as she put them on and refused to come in from playing when called. She hated the khaki uniform Martha had bought her and no matter how much she tried, couldn't seem to wear it out. Using her bare hands, the eight-year-old attempted to tear the fabric to make it look worn. When that didn't work, she found a razor blade, stretched the uniform and sliced a long line through it. She went on to cut another round hole on one of the green leather dining room chairs that had just been delivered that day.

"Who did this?" Martha shrieked when she came home from work and spied the fresh slashes in the seat of her beautiful, brand-new chair. "Rosemary! Did you do this?"

Rosemary simply nodded, not feeling the least bit guilty for ridding herself of the ugly khaki dress.

Despite the razor blade incident, Martha was convinced that her little sister was destined for greatness. In the way she cared for the children, in her interactions with the other villagers, in her approach to study and prayer, Rosemary showed a depth of compassion, kindness and wisdom that made her seem much older than her years. She excelled in everything she attempted, from sports to spirituality, even surpassing her brothers in her academic pursuits.

Martha's husband, too, recognized something different about Rose, something even his own children lacked. Now the headmaster at Rosemary's school, Geraldo had heard from her third-grade teacher that she was very smart, smarter than most of the students in her class. He decided to discreetly follow her and see for himself. Rosemary sensed he was keeping an eye on her but didn't know why.

That night he told Martha, "This child is very clever. She learns very quickly and remembers what she reads. And she is a natural leader with the other children. She knows how to motivate them to do what she wants. She will grow up to be somebody one day."

Rosemary had been sitting nearby, close enough to hear pieces of the conversation. She had no idea what it meant to "be somebody," but that, she vowed, is exactly what she would be.

CHAPTER TWO

TOUGH AND READY

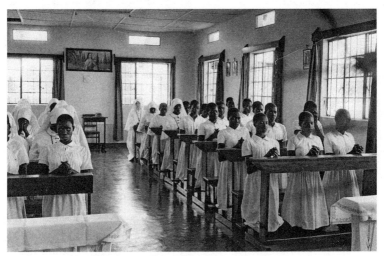

New girls joining Sacred Heart Sisters Convent in Moyo, 1972

The boys at school seemed never to tire of teasing Rosemary and the other girls. The teacher's seating assignment—a boy on either side of each girl—was, for many, a recipe for disaster. At every opportunity, the mischief-makers reached rudely across the young women, shoved them out of the way, and spoke loudly and close to their ears. Their behavior, including the habit of making fun of female students whose menstrual periods happened to start during class, when no

---

sanitary napkins were available, was so embarrassing and offensive that several girls dropped out of school because of it.

Like some of them, Rosemary had previously attended an all-girl school, excelling as the best in her class, particularly in English, and often leading her classmates in prayer and traditional African dances. After three years, she was transferred to the co-ed facility in Paidha, where the boys constantly tried to distract her with their bullying. Unlike some of her friends, however, she had grown up with three older brothers, playing football—not the more forgiving netball, like girls usually played, but the rough-and-tumble game of grown men—and running and jumping boisterously right along with them. Still, she had never picked a fight in the village, nor responded by lashing out at her tormenters, and was in fact known for her lighthearted demeanor and ability to laugh even when others were behaving badly.

One day before class, her brother Luigi, who was only one year ahead of her in school, walked past Rosemary's desk in the back of the room and noticed that something was wrong. His usually outgoing sister had scooted back in her chair, hands in her lap. She was fighting back tears.

"Rosemary, what's happening? You are very quiet, not like yourself. What's the matter?"

"That boy knocked my head," she replied, pointing to the culprit, who had taken his seat in one of the front rows.

"Walk with me," Luigi said, leading her out the door. "Now show me what he did to you."

Standing close to her brother, Rosemary balled up her fist and thumped him on the head.

Luigi's eyes widened. "Okay, we're going back in. And you're going to do to him exactly what he did to you."

Back in the classroom, Rosemary headed straight for the boy, drew back her fist and knocked him as hard as she could. Startled, the boy rubbed his smarting jaw as she walked back to her seat.

After that, she knew what she had to do. One day, a male classmate charged into the room and, amid shrieks of laughter, deliberately fell into Rosemary's lap while she was reading. The boy was on the small side, not particularly strong but always surrounded by friends who were stronger and tougher than he. Without hesitation, the little girl with the big smile began to pummel the bully, on his face, his arm, his chest, until he fell to the floor.

Geraldo, Rosemary's brother-in-law and now the head teacher at her school, happened to enter the room just as it erupted in chaos. "What's happening here? What's going on?" he demanded.

"She did it! She did it!" the kids yelled, unable to contain their excitement. "Look! Rose has beaten this boy and he has collapsed."

Geraldo stifled the urge to grin, turning instead to Rosemary. "Get out of this class and go home. You can't come back for two weeks. That is your punishment for hurting this boy."

Rosemary gathered her books, held her head high and strolled out of the room. Then she walked to her parents' house and explained to her father, "This boy was disturbing me and now I'm being punished. I would like to you to go to the school and plead on my behalf."

Finding it difficult to refuse his youngest daughter, Martino talked Geraldo into reducing Rosemary's sentence to one week. She later became the school prefect, a sort of hall monitor responsible for helping maintain order among the students. Thanks to an odd twist of fate, she now had the authority to punish the boys if they were late for school or talked in class. She had no qualms about doing just that.

Rosemary's first glimpse of political violence came in 1964. She was too young to understand why people were running from nearby Congo to Uganda, with nothing but the clothes they were wearing, to escape the air strikes led by U.S. and Belgian forces in an attempt to flush out a Congolese rebel faction terrorizing the eastern part of the country. More than once, she witnessed bombs soaring through the sky—evil, frightening fireworks that made no sense to an eight-year-old girl. It was the first time young Rosemary had heard of the rebel activities, or even real, grown-up war.

As always, her parents showed warmth and compassion to those most in need, harboring so many Congolese refugees that they lost count of the strangers living in their home. Martha did the same thing, cooking enormous meals for the hungry and showing Rosemary, by her example, why it was important to care for large groups of people in crisis.

That year, Rosemary and her family were forced, for the first time, to leave and take shelter elsewhere, far from home. While sleeping outside, exposed to the elements, the girl contracted pneumonia, prompting Sabina to brave the danger and return with her daughter to seek medical treatment in their home village.

When she was thirteen, Rosemary's parents called her back to live in their house. On the heels of the Congo Crisis, as it came to be known, life became peaceful again. Then in 1971, Ugandan Armed Forces Commander Idi Amin overthrew his former cohort, Prime Minister Milton Obote, in a military coup, and declared himself President of Uganda. Amin's rule was riddled with human rights abuses, ethnic persecution and senseless killings, including that of Rosemary's cousin Isaiah, an active supporter of the Democratic Party. Stubborn and staunchly committed to the Pope, Isaiah held fast to his convictions despite the fact that Amin was determined to abolish all existing political parties and eliminate anyone who belonged to them.

One day, Isaiah announced his intentions to go to a public rally in Nebbi, approximately fifteen kilometers east of Paidha, where Amin was scheduled to speak.

"Isaiah, please don't go," his wife begged. "People don't talk well about you. Something may happen."

But he had already made up his mind. Heavily guarded, Amin was addressing the crowd when, under specific orders from the president, soldiers singled Isaiah out, dragged him

away from the rally and drove with him northwest toward
Arua. One of Rosemary's uncles, a strong supporter of the
Uganda People's Congress, was oddly jubilant when he
delivered the news of the young man's death to Sabina.

Soon after, Rosemary watched in horror as a stranger burst
into the family home and began chasing her mother with an ax.
"We will eliminate all the people who belong to the Democratic
party!" the man shouted as Sabina ran to the back of the house.
"We will eliminate you and your family!" Managing to escape,
Rosemary's mother fled to her childhood home in Congo,
where she stayed for some time. She returned with a newfound
sense of courage, telling her family, "I must go and see with my
own eyes if the son of my sister is killed. If he is dead, perhaps
they will give me permission to take the body."

"Mother, be careful," her older children warned. "You are
not safe."

Rosemary was too young to understand the details, but
when her mother returned, she was empty-handed. Isaiah's
corpse was later stolen from his captors, loaded onto a truck and
buried without benefit of a funeral. He had been slaughtered
with a knife, parts of his body mutilated beyond recognition.

From her friends and family, Rosemary heard stories about
other murders. By most accounts, by the time Amin's reign
of terror ended in 1979, he and his mercenaries had killed an
estimated 300,000 of the country's twelve million people, and
many more had been forced to flee for their lives.

Rosemary's sense of safety was rattled but one conviction
stood strong. Devout Catholics, Rosemary's parents never

failed to pray with their children each evening. Long before entering catechism class, the little girl had learned from her brothers how to say the rosary, kneeling in prayerful reflection and counting the beads one by one. Living so close to the local parish, Rosemary found that praying there each morning was a natural way to begin the day, so she tried to hurry her housework so as not to be late for Mass.

Aware that her sister Martha had at one time yearned to join a convent and that her brother Valerio had set out on a short-lived quest to become a priest but later dropped out of seminary, Rosemary instinctively knew that, if one felt a higher calling to devote one's life to God, there was a place in which to do so. But the only nuns she knew were Sisters from Gulu, east of Paidha, who had taught in the primary schools and worked in the missions when she was a child and not yet able to appreciate their service. Then she heard about the Sisters from neighboring Sudan who were caring for the poor and the orphaned, and the tug in her heart told her everything she needed to know. Here was a way to help other people, those who had no one else to inspire or love them unconditionally. Here was a mission that resonated deep within her soul. Here was the thing she was meant to do.

"Mother," fifteen-year-old Rosemary said one day on the way to market, "I'm going to join the convent."

CHAPTER THREE

SISTER, NOT SAINT

Fourteen-year-old Sister Rosemary in theatre performance

"What?!" Rosemary's brothers did not respond favorably when they learned of her plans to become a nun. "Are you joking?"

"Why are you doing this?" Valerio argued. "Is it because you saw that other girl in the village join the convent? There's no need for you to do what she did. You're too young."

"Let her go," her father Martino interrupted. "She is a wise girl. Let her decide what she wants to do."

Her mother Sabina accepted her decision too, as did her sisters. Martha, who identified most with Rosemary's calling because she had held similar aspirations at one time, advised her to follow her heart and shushed their brothers when they berated her. A year later, Martha would be the one to travel to the convent in Moyo, 150 miles northeast of Paidha, to watch her little sister take the first official step in becoming a Sister.

Mindful of Valerio's failure to follow through with the priesthood, Catherine urged Rosemary, "Now that you are going to the convent, please don't shame our family by leaving. Follow your vocation and stay with it, because our parents have given you to God."

But Rosemary's brothers refused to support her and on that March day in 1972, as she was packing to leave, they attempted to lock her out of the house so she couldn't get to her dresses. Frustrated with his sons' obstinance, her father shattered a window and motioned to Rosemary, "Get your things and let's go."

The convent in Moyo, a small town near the Sudan border, appeared much older than it actually was. Built in the 1960s as a teacher-training center, it had sheltered a congregation of displaced Sudanese nuns who settled in Uganda after fleeing the war zone in southern Sudan. The Sisters of the Sacred Heart of Jesus beautified the dilapidated buildings as best they could, forming classrooms and worship areas that were better suited for nuns in training and building a few new ones with their own muscle, hard work and sweat. They now referred to the school as the Mother House.

Rosemary had never seen so many nuns—most were, in fact, still candidates for the Sisterhood—together in one place. There were girls from the Sudan, from other parts of Uganda, from cultures she knew nothing about, speaking dialects she'd never heard. She watched them scurry from one room to another, all dressed in white uniforms, and it suddenly occurred to her that she had never lived in a place with no men. For the first time in her life, she was totally separated from her family, with only the promise of rare trips home and infrequent visits from her sisters as she completed the rigorous, four-year process from candidate to postulant to novice and, finally, nun. At fifteen, she was the youngest girl in the convent.

The Sisters in charge were friendly and welcoming, but life among Catholic nuns was no easy adjustment for Rosemary, who was used to being coddled as the last-born girl in her family. The nunnery was much different from her own lively household, where self-expression was encouraged, and it took Rosemary a while to settle in and find her place among strangers.

Each new candidate, or aspirant, was assigned a senior Sister to serve as a mother figure, mentor and spiritual leader and keenly follow the candidate's progress and character formation throughout her years at the convent. Sister Anita, who was in charge of the aspirants, became Rosemary's constant shadow, observing her, offering guidance and, whenever possible, bending the rules for the compound's youngest resident.

Having been spoiled by her parents and siblings, Rosemary found it difficult to adhere to the strict standards of religious life. After lunch, she struggled to stay awake during spiritual readings and often fell asleep when she was supposed to be listening to the Sister in charge. She loved to pray but hated getting up at 6:00 every morning to attend church. "Why must I do this?" she asked herself, struggling to drag herself out of bed at such an early hour. "I see only darkness, no sunshine. Am I going to do this all my life? I don't think I can bear it."

Sister Anita repeatedly scolded the teenager for oversleeping, but it was of no use. One day, as Rosemary lay in her bed, sound asleep with her roommates already gathering at Mass, the Sister lightly touched her arm in an effort to wake her.

Rosemary screamed and bolted upright in bed. "Please don't touch me if you want to wake me up," she said, rubbing her eyes. "Just call my name, even in the middle of the night, but don't touch me. I get scared when you do that."

"I think you need to let this little girl sleep a bit more," Sister Anita told the Mother Superior General, a kind Italian nun named Elizabeth. "She needs the sleep."

Sensing that Rosemary was, in many ways, still a child, Mother Elizabeth called the girl to her office. "Rosemary," she said, "for your punishment, you will not join the others at daybreak but will remain sleeping and go to the main church later, by yourself."

The "punishment," for Rosemary, was a blessing in disguise, and she silently thanked her superiors for the discipline she deserved.

Rosemary loved beautiful things and was truly surprised when she was asked to give up some of her most prized belongings. Naïve in the ways of the religious world, she expected to wear the same clothing, the same jewelry, the same hairstyle she had embraced in the secular life she had left far behind.

Before leaving for the convent, her sister had plaited her long, beautiful hair into a thick Afro. But the other girls wore their hair short.

"Rosemary, we must find a way to shorten your hair," Mother Elizabeth told her one day after church. "When you sit in the front pew, your hair is so big that you block the view for everyone else."

"But I don't want my hair to be short," Rosemary protested. "No one has ever cut my hair. They always braid it at home."

"Well you're not home any more." Mother Elizabeth paused for a moment, then added, "All right, we'll just trim it. Okay?"

By the time the nuns cropped Rosemary's hair, it was nearly as short as the other girls'. She pouted for a whole week—this was a terrible sacrifice, surrendering her personal beauty—but she eventually learned to live with her new style.

Giving up her colorful dresses and the small green purse she had made for herself was no less frustrating. After their morning baths, the aspirants would dress in uniforms—gray for casual times, white for official church events—stored in a common dressing room. Everyone wore the same thing—just two drab colors, no purple, no orange, no green. "Why must you take all my dresses?" she asked as the nuns gathered them upon her arrival. "Can't I keep this one? What about that?"

"No, Rosemary, this is not what we wear here. You must give up your worldly possessions and dress in a manner becoming of a servant of God."

Mother Elizabeth quickly developed a tender spot in her heart for Rosemary and was careful not to be too hard on the girl given her young age and small stature. But there was one more thing that must go.

"Rosemary, it's time for us to remove these," said the Superior, wielding a pair of scissors. Little by little, she began to cut away the long line of beaded bracelets encircling Rosemary's arm, for they were too tight to slip over the girl's wrist. With every snip, Mother Elizabeth reassured the anxious Rosemary with her kind words, until by the time the very last ringlet was gone, the young candidate had vowed to herself, "Okay, if this is the life I want, I will have to accept what it brings."

One thing she never accepted was the afternoon ritual of taking tea, a holdover from the days before Uganda gained independence from Britain in 1962. Whatever you have on your plate, whatever you have in your cup, you must finish, the girls were told, because there are people suffering around the world who do not have enough to eat or drink. Each day, those in charge of food preparation brought teapots from the common area and filled the cups of their peers, but Rosemary would only take a few sips and leave the rest to grow cold. She had always been a poor eater anyway and to her, the beverage tasted like dirty water.

"Rosemary, we always find tea in your cup," Sister Anita corrected. "That's not nice. You're wasting food and it is not right. You must finish everything you are given."

"But I don't know how to take tea," Rosemary said, remembering her father's strong java brew and wondering if perhaps she could ask for smaller plates and cups. "I would like coffee instead."

Sister Anita wrinkled her brow. "We do not serve coffee here. So you will have to learn to drink tea."

Rosemary held her nose and swallowed until it was gone. For now, she would obey her superiors. Four years later, when she took her solemn vows as a Sister, she would resume her beloved coffee drinking.

Firm but understanding, the Sisters showed sensitivity in the household tasks they required of little Rosemary. Like her fellow aspirants, she was expected to follow a daily routine of service and gratitude while keeping the house clean and tending the grounds. With no hired help to maintain the compound, cook meals or provide ready-made clothing and supplies, it was critical that the girls learn to be self-sufficient and develop a strong work ethic in order to survive.

Rosemary's primary chore was watering, from one end of the property to the other, the groves of lemon and orange trees, and the flower gardens. Hers, she knew, was a much lighter assignment than most.

To amuse herself, the jovial girl would sing as loudly as she could while moving from one plant to another with the water hose. Her favorite hymn was *Veni Creator Spiritus*, the Song of the Holy Spirit, which she would spontaneously belt out each time the words popped into her mind: *Veni, creator*

Spiritus, mentes tuorum visita; imple superna gratia, quae tu creasti pectora. Come, Holy Ghost, Creator blest, and in our hearts take up Thy rest; come with Thy grace and heav'nly aid, to fill the hearts which Thou hast made.

"Rosemary, what is all this noise? You're disturbing the other girls," the Sisters scolded. "When you're working, you must be quiet. This is a time to remain silent. Don't sing or talk."

For the most part, Rosemary's overwhelming fear of caterpillars, with their big, staring eyes, kept her out of the vegetable gardens but she learned to prune the grapevines to keep them healthy so the Sisters could produce up to 200 liters of red wine each year. In the nearby forest, she gathered firewood and chopped it into small pieces with which to stoke the oven. One time, Rosemary and another girl, Seraphine, were sorting groundnuts in the shed when a caterpillar crawled past her feet. Terrified, Rosemary jumped, but Seraphine, unafraid and seizing the chance to tease her friend, broke a long twig, scooped up the larva, and brandished the creature in Rosemary's face. Running as fast as she could, Rosemary didn't stop until she reached the nearest classroom, where a priest was instructing a group of novices.

Irritated, he glanced up to see who had caused the interruption. "Rosemary, what is your problem?"

"Seraphine," she panted, "is chasing me with a caterpillar." The priest barely managed to curb the smile tickling the corners of his mouth.

In spite of her phobia, it was a different creature, one that Rosemary couldn't see, that posed the real danger. One Sunday evening soon after she joined the novitiate—a period that lasts two years before one is allowed to take her religious vows—she and the other novices set out to fetch water from a bore hole a few meters outside the convent. The only well in the area, it frequently drew long lines of women and girls, who often waited more than three hours to fill their buckets. Since the Sacred Heart novices would miss valuable training time if they waited in line, the Sister in charge sent them at night when the other villagers were sleeping.

Passing the convent gate in the dark, with no flashlight to guide her way, Rosemary felt a sharp pain in her right foot, as if it had been pricked by a needle or scratched by a sharp stick. By the time she reached the well a few minutes later, the pain had intensified and moved to the joints in her body.

"I don't feel well," she told her friends. "I hurt all over. Something is wrong."

Moments later, she collapsed. "A snake must have bitten Rosemary," the other novices concluded as they hurriedly carried her home and explained to the Sister in charge. Immediately, she was transported to a nearby clinic run by the Comboni Missionary Sisters. After listening to the girls recount what they had seen, a kind Italian nun named Alexandrina administered a series of antibiotic shots and tied a smooth, dark object to the site of the snakebite.

In African culture, the "black stone"—in actuality, it is not a rock but an animal bone fired with coal until black and shiny—is believed to absorb and neutralize the deadly effects of snake venom. Sometimes called a Belgian stone, it is used in tribal medicine, as an emergency home remedy, and as a treatment in hospitals and health centers across the continent.

All night, the pain was so great that Rosemary thought she was surely going to die. A large swelling in her throat made it difficult to breathe.

The next morning she woke with a swollen foot, and it was weeks before she could walk well again. Rather than fear snakes after that, she grew determined to kill them whenever they crossed her path. She would have more than one opportunity to do so.

One of Rosemary's favorite tasks was learning to bake biscuits, cakes and loaves of bread. She was especially proud of this accomplishment, as she was the only girl chosen to travel to an Italian convent to study the art of baking with the nuns there.

Sewing was another strong point for Rosemary, who taught herself how to use the foot-pedal machines. Her tailoring and needlework skills were superb and before long she was sewing dresses, bras and traditional dance and feast costumes for the rest of the girls.

Many of the activities at the convent were designed not just to teach the importance of discipline and prayer, but to get the candidates accustomed to living with others, cultivate selflessness and community spirit, and enable them to empathize and work for the common good of people from all walks of life, without grumbling. At the end of each day the girls threw their dirty clothes into a common laundry room. Then, one day a week, they systematically gathered as a group to soap, rinse and hang all the clothes, not just their own. The next day, the girls checked for torn seams, repaired uniforms that needed attention, and ironed and folded them into neat piles to be distributed among the residents. Life at the convent offered few luxuries, but the candidates learned to care for what they had and make their belongings last well beyond the point at which more affluent people would have thrown them away.

After a while, Rosemary rarely quibbled about hard work or the tasks she was given, so the nuns were surprised when the young aspirant balked at the idea of caring for the German shepherds that had taken up residence at the convent.

"Oh no, I can't," she said. "Something bad will happen to me if I do. I will die, or my parents will die."

Mother Elizabeth was clearly puzzled. "Rosemary, that is silly. The dogs can't hurt you. It is your job now to take care of them and make sure they are fed."

To Rosemary, who had grown up hearing her grandfather's story, over and over, this was an impossible request. One of her uncles, she was told as a child, had loved his dog very much. The dog loved him back, so much so that when the man died, at the funeral the animal jumped on his casket as if to be buried with him. That day, Rosemary's grandfather declared, "This is a bad omen. From this day onward, no one in this family will keep dogs."

Worried, the young novice decided to ignore her superior's instructions rather than risk the wrath of her family. Seeing the dogs' empty bowl, Mother Elizabeth called the girl to her office.

"Rosemary, have the dogs eaten today?"

"No, Mother, they have not." Embarrassed, Rosemary chose not to explain why she was so afraid of the dogs.

"Why didn't you feed them? You must know what it feels like to be hungry. They get hungry too."

"But I can't," Rosemary whined.

"Yes, you can. In fact, you will look after these dogs, and do it well, for one year."

Defeated, Rosemary did as she was told. Day after day, she fed and left water for Bombo and Beauty, keeping her distance when they wagged their tails or tried to get near her. To her great surprise, her fears gradually eased and one day she ventured closer while still refusing to touch them. Within a few weeks, she was petting the grateful canines and throwing sticks for them to catch.

One day she approached Mother Elizabeth with a request of her own. "I would like a new towel for the dogs' bed, and some flea powder. And I need some wheat flour to cook biscuits for them so they can eat well."

"What?" the nun said. "I thought you didn't like the dogs."

"I changed my mind. I need these things to care for them."

"Rosemary, you are far too demanding," the superior said. "I will give you the towel and the powder. But I will not give you any flour to cook for them. That is a waste of our resources."

Later that day, when her baking duties were finished, Rosemary remained in the kitchen, closing the door. Retrieving a bag of flour from the cupboard, she hurried to bake a pan of biscuits for her four-legged friends, hoping no one would detect the aroma wafting from the oven.

She continued to sneak biscuits, cakes and other treats to the dogs and, upon becoming a postulant at the end of her first year, asked permission to keep caring for Bombo and Beauty. She continued until she became a novice, another year after that. By that time, she knew in her heart that long-held superstitions, no matter how ingrained, can be overcome.

Over time, Rosemary grew more comfortable with her new life at the convent. Prayer, she would slowly come to understand, is an art one must learn.

Father, what is this all about? she prayed as she sat in the chapel and contemplated her calling. *What would you have me do with my life?*

Months passed, and she began to meditate with more focus, more intention, seeking answers to specific questions and concerns. Spiritual reflection became a natural part of her day.

The girls at the convent worked hard, but they were also allowed time to play. They were, after all, still children with pent-up energy that needed to be released. Rosemary learned how to play the piano, but she liked football more. Just like in Paidha, the compound's female residents played netball, a modified version of American basketball. A fast runner and quick to catch the ball, the athletic Rosemary played center, defending both sides of the court. Sometimes, however, she missed playing football with her brothers and, when no one else was around, would kick the netball like a pigskin.

The Sisters noticed, too, that Rosemary's organizational skills were superb despite her young age. Even more impressive, perhaps, was her memory, which was extraordinarily sharp—so sharp, in fact, that she quickly mastered all her new classes and assignments, no matter how difficult.

"Rosemary, we are putting you in charge of our concerts and dramas," Sister Terezina, the novice mistress, announced one day. "We want you to direct them from now on."

Staged in the convent's common recreation room, the classical plays had not always gone smoothly. It was no easy task to manage a bunch of novices and postulants with no prior acting experience, but Rosemary found a way. Before leading each new Shakespearean drama, she read the entire book, studied the parts and scribbled copious notes about how to proceed. When the "cast" gathered for their first practice, she paired the girls with their roles and gave them precise instructions on how to speak and where to stand. No matter how badly they fumbled their lines, she always seemed to remember what they had forgotten and nudge them back on track—with or without the written script.

"Rosemary, you have the brain of an elephant," one of the nuns remarked. "How do you recall everything without the papers in front of you?"

Rosemary shrugged. She had memorized every part, line by line. It was as if they were stamped in her brain.

Tough but kindhearted, Mother Elizabeth came to favor Rosemary so much that she sometimes took the girl with her when she traveled. In Rosemary's first year as a postulant, she even drove the girl to Martha's house to visit with her mother and sisters. On that occasion, Catherine asked, "Are you still determined to become a nun? You can come back and continue your studies here if you change your mind."

"No," Rosemary said, assuring her family that she was all right and not lacking for anything. "I want to continue."

On one of their journeys together, the Mother Superior handed Rosemary her habit to press.

"But Mother Elizabeth, I've never ironed a habit before."

"Rosemary," she said, "I trust you. Whatever you do, it is always the best."

Mother Elizabeth eventually left for Italy, and Mother Annetta became the first African Superior General in the Sacred Heart congregation. Elizabeth had been such an important role model that, in 1989, when Rosemary started a vocational training group to teach the women of Moyo how to read and write, she named it Saint Elizabeth Women's Group.

Some of the girls at the Moyo convent lagged behind in their religious studies and weren't ready to take their final vows in four years. As usual, Rosemary excelled in everything she did and by the time she was nineteen, she had completed the entire process and had begun preparing for the ceremony. But there was one problem: A novice must be at least twenty years old to become a nun.

Once Rosemary set her mind to do something, though, there was no turning back. Determination was a trait that had served her well, most of the time, and it would continue to do so.

At the end of the two-year novitiate phase, Rosemary and ten other girls were accepted to take their first vows. Each was given a perfectly-tailored habit—white with a red embroidered cross, red collar and red buttons, one for each of the six vows: chastity, poverty, obedience, love, zeal and humility—to wear on the day they were to be sworn in as nuns.

Hoping no one would notice, she never mentioned her age. A month later, when Rosemary was about to receive her first assignment, she answered a call from Mother Annetta, the new Mother Superior. "Rosemary, you know you are under age. You should not have taken the vows. You cannot take them if you are only nineteen."

"I know," the young woman admitted. "But it's too late now. I am ready to work for the people."

CHAPTER FOUR

STITCHES

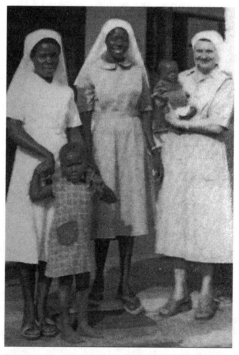

Sister Rosemary at the Moyo Mission Dispensary in 1980

Mother Annetta sent Rosemary and two other new Sisters, Seraphine and Pierina, to the Angal Hospital, a small facility run by the Italian Comboni Sisters in Uganda's West Nile region, to gain firsthand experience in helping the sick. On her first day, Rosemary was assigned to a maternity ward, where she learned to deliver babies with the help of trained midwives. Having spent much of her young life caring for children, she fell in love with the infants and the new mothers and quickly took on a leadership role in the ward. At the end of the year, Rosemary had demonstrated such a natural ability for delivering babies that the Comboni Sisters recommended she go to the Kalongo School of Nursing and Midwifery in the Gulu District.

Dr. Ambrosoli, the Italian surgeon who founded the community hospital affiliated with the midwifery school, noticed how quickly she mastered her biology, anatomy and physiology class, even though she had no prior knowledge of the topics, and sensed she would be an able apprentice. "I would like Rosemary to work with me in the operating theater," he told her teacher soon after her training began. In order to assist him, however, Sister Rosemary would have to give up her ministry class, a sacrifice she gladly made in exchange for the opportunity to gain practical experience. She had no idea how critical it would become in the days ahead.

The hard-working priest-doctor performed surgeries at the Kalongo hospital each day from 8:00 in the morning until 1:00 in the afternoon. "Rosemary, you finish," he would say at the close of each operation. From the surgeon Rosemary learned how to stitch incisions as skillfully, and with as much reverence, as she would a special religious uniform. In her usual quick-study method, she learned to distinguish which type of needle—round, l-shaped, cutting—to use for which vessel or muscle, and how to handle a *klamar*, a kind of toothless scissor for holding blood vessels steady.

Sister Rosemary, too, remained steady, bracing herself against the initial nausea and the smell of flesh burning under the surgeon's white-hot, sealing cauterization iron. Her habit of eating very little meat, and very little food overall—for energy, she drank only one glass of milk with raw eggs each day—helped quiet her stomach as she focused on closing the bleeding points. Before long, the queasiness subsided, as one after another, she assisted with Caesarean sections, bone surgeries and treatments for infant and adult hydrocele, a fluid-filled sac in the scrotum that causes it to swell.

Her work continued on weekends, when Dr. Ambrosoli performed delicate cataract procedures requiring tiny needles. Rosemary was in charge of threading each one with lightning speed.

"Rosemary, you have the eyes of a witch doctor," he teased. "You will be very useful one day wherever you work."

She enjoyed her surgical experience so much that, had her life not taken a dramatic turn a few years later, she might well have become a nurse or even a paramedic. She had already jumped at the chance to study midwifery, a field that suited her patient, nurturing disposition. She loved delivering babies— helping a woman give birth and holding the child immediately afterward made her heart soar—but her favorite part was spending time in the nursery, hovering over the smallest infants at risk of death and needing round-the-clock care. In

1980, four years after she completed her religious studies, she earned her certification as a midwife and in 1981 she arrived at her first official post, a primitive medical clinic in Moyo.

Guerilla warfare had left the town nearly deserted. After the removal of Idi Amin in 1979, the disparate groups that had helped bring him down fought fiercely for control of Uganda, leaving civilians caught in the middle. The remnants of Amin's supporters formed rebel groups in the West Nile region while other militia descended on the southwest part of the country. The actions of both resulted in genocide, the establishment of refugee camps under military control, and untold human rights abuses. The National Resistance Army, which waged war on the government of President Milton Obote, recruited a number of child soldiers, even after it morphed into the country's official army. During the siege in northern Uganda, many Moyo residents had fled to safety in nearby Sudan, and government soldiers—Acholi natives who later joined Joseph Kony's Lord's Resistance Army—now patrolled the streets. It was often hard to tell the insurgents from the real officers.

A group of Comboni Sisters had just left the mission, handing over the reins to the order of the Sacred Heart of Jesus. It never occurred to Sister Rosemary that she would be running the dispensary with no doctor and, upon the departure of the last remaining Italian Sister the next year, by herself. The responsibility didn't bother Rosemary, but navigating the swarm of soldiers on her way to the clinic frightened her, especially at night. To her credit, she was able to speak the local

Madi and *Luo* dialects, which allowed her to communicate with both patients and soldiers, who were often one and the same.

Medicines, mostly left behind by the Comboni Sisters, were always in short supply at the dispensary, and with no electricity, the clinic relied on sunshine during the day and kerosene lamps at night to provide light for emergency procedures. Sister Rosemary's prior experience as assistant to the priest-surgeon Dr. Ambrosoli proved invaluable, as she already knew the best ways to stop bleeding and the importance of antibiotic injections to ward off infection. The only medical provider in town—the nearest hospital was many miles away— she found herself delivering babies at all hours and performing minor operations on the spot. With most of the villagers still hiding in Sudan, the majority of her patients were soldiers and their wives.

Not easily discouraged, Sister Rosemary worked tirelessly, facing hardships and tasks with a strength beyond her years and treating her patients, regardless of status or background, in a loving, down-to-earth way. The villagers came to know her as someone they could count on, someone who would respect and care for them in their moments of crisis and pain. Once, when a woman was having difficulty giving birth, Rosemary used a vacuum to extract the eight-pound, six-ounce baby, nursed the mother for more than a week, and sent them both home in good health.

In addition to running the dispensary, Sister Rosemary was charged with reviving the adjacent orphanage, constructed in 1947 by the Comboni missionaries and now filled with children hurriedly dropped off by panicked Moyo residents en route to Sudan or orphaned when the rebels killed their parents. Some arrived via military truck, alone and abandoned by family members. There were one-day-old babies, wide-eyed toddlers, and five-year-olds whose parents had tried to murder them so as not to be burdened with feeding them. All were considered throwaways. No one seemed to know what to do with them—no one except a diminutive Catholic nun with an enormous heart. Rosemary took each one under her wing, raising them as if they were her own and moving from the convent into a house closer to the orphanage to be near them at night.

Under her direction, the babies' home grew in size and gained a reputation as one of the best in northern Uganda. People from other villages began to bring children whose mothers had died in childbirth or fallen victim to the growing AIDS epidemic, spurring the Sacred Heart Sisters to further their mission of tending to the weakest of the weak.

Coincidentally, the Moyo clinic was the same one where Rosemary had been treated for snakebite during her first year as a novice. One morning, as she opened the door to the "store"— one of the free rooms that warehoused food for the orphans— she sensed a gentle movement in the exposed timbers of the ceiling. Curious, she looked up to see an enormous brown snake crawling on the wooden beams above her head.

"What should we do?" she asked after summoning a few of the women who worked in the orphanage.

They suggested she call one of the guards to come shoot the snake. But when the man saw the reptile, he simply shrugged. "It is not possible for you to aim correctly from here," he told Sister Rose. "You will have to leave that thing alone."

Not sure if her plan would work but determined to kill the intruder by any means possible and keep the children safe, Rosemary gathered a few rugged stones from the yard. She missed the snake on her first throw, but the second one, delivered with more boldness and an accuracy mustered from her childhood stone-tossing days, landed square on its thick body, knocking it to the floor. Unfazed, Sister Rosemary grabbed a stick and beat the creature until it was dead.

Soon after his ordination, a young Father named Gabaglio Luigi was assigned to Moyo to replace Father Bilbao, a much-loved parish priest who had been killed in an ambush in Kampala. The villagers expected much of Father Luigi, who didn't understand the *Madi* language and felt uneasy about filling the former priest's larger-than-life shoes. Adding to his discomfort was the fact that, despite his lack of experience in working with women, he was now in charge of the parish and expected to aid the Sisters in the mission. Sister Rosemary welcomed him with open arms, patiently listened to his suggestions, even if they were far-fetched, and gave him the encouragement he needed in the first months of his priesthood. Despite his newfound confidence, however, he was not cut out for the operating room.

"Help us! Help us!"

The words rang loudly through the dispensary. Sister Rosemary looked up to see a woman struggling to stand while supporting the weight of the two young men clinging to her shoulders. Blood ran in streams from their bodies, their torsos riddled with wounds like those that might have been inflicted by a firing squad.

"Help us! Help us!" the mother cried. "Someone threw a grenade through our window! Please help us!"

Sister Rosemary grabbed a wad of rags and began to apply makeshift tourniquets. With no medical personnel to assist her, she quickly instructed the Sisters to gather more strips of cloth and summon Father Luigi. At least he could hold the hurricane lamp while she removed the shrapnel embedded by the explosion.

"Father, I need you to hold this steady for me," she said calmly as the priest entered the room. "We must save the lives of these brothers. Without us, they will die."

Dipping her bare fingers in antiseptic, Rosemary began digging in the open, bloody wounds to remove the splinters, just as she had during her apprenticeship at the Kalongo hospital. Father Luigi's face grew pale and he started to teeter on his feet.

"Are you all right?"

"I'm not sure," he whispered, the lamp swaying from side to side as he stumbled.

"Take him out and find me someone else," Rosemary directed the Sisters. "The Father is about to faint."

To the boys' mother, she offered more realism than hope: "If they do not die within the next twelve hours, they will live." All night, the two women kept watch by the patients' bedside and in the morning, the young men woke from a deep sleep. They were soon back at home with their mother.

Sister Rosemary ran the Moyo dispensary for three years and, in 1985, was transferred to a different clinic in the small town of Adjumani, about twenty miles to the south. Yearning to become a paramedic so she could be of more service to her people, at the end of the year she asked her Superiors to let her finish her secondary studies at Sacred Heart School in Gulu, the largest town in northern Uganda. Those plans would abruptly change a few weeks later with the outbreak of another civil war, this one even more brutal and senseless than the last.

CHAPTER FIVE

CAUGHT IN THE CROSSFIRE

JOSEPH KONY

Sister Rosemary woke to the din of loud singing and the scrape of metal banging against metal. Tumbling out of bed and slipping her feet into a pair of flat shoes, she grabbed a robe and headed for the main door. In her haste, she nearly ran into Sisters Devota, Alice and Lily Grace.

"Sister Rosemary! What's happening?"

"Shhh! I don't know," Rosemary replied, prying open the door just enough to peer outside. The noise appeared to be coming from down the street but amid all the commotion, it was hard to tell exactly what was going on.

It wasn't until the next morning, when the word spread through the heart of Gulu, that the mystery was solved or, depending on how one interpreted it, muddied even more. A group of insurgents, filled with rebellious courage in the presence of the government soldiers, had gathered to sing and shout through the streets while beating empty tin cans to create as much racket as possible. Their leader, Sister Rosemary learned, was a woman named Alice Lakwena.

Born Alice Auma, the Acholi native had reportedly been possessed by the spirit of Lakwena, a dead Italian Army officer, while working as a spirit-medium near Gulu. She claimed that the ghost had ordered her to launch the Holy Spirit Movement and lead the Acholi people to overthrow the government of the new president, Yoweri Museveni, who had helped depose both Idi Amin in 1979 and Milton Obote in 1985, the same year Sister Rosemary Nyirumbe arrived at the Sacred Heart School in Gulu. Lakwena and her supporters accused Museveni, a Southerner, of being unjust to the people of northern Uganda.

In 1987, Lakwena left Acholiland, leading thousands of believers south toward Kampala. She was defeated by Museveni's troops and forced into exile, but by then a new leader had emerged in northern Uganda.

A slight man whose dark, deep-set eyes had once earned him the nickname "Black Monkey," Joseph Kony recruited a number of Acholi tribesmen and others who bore grudges against Museveni for stealing their political power, all while claiming to be Lakwena's cousin and convincing his followers that he had been chosen to rebuild the Acholi nation in keeping with the Biblical Ten Commandments. Under Kony's guidance, members of the newly formed rebel group known as the Lord's Resistance Army set out on a violent mission, looting homes, terrorizing civilians, torching villages, ambushing buses, and raping, murdering and mutilating victims at random. When he failed to recruit enough adult males, he resorted to kidnapping children. Over the next twenty years, LRA soldiers, most of them organized into squads of ten or twenty, snatched thousands of youth—by some estimates, up to 30,000—from their homes and schools, killing their families and teachers and forcing them to fight in his Army. Boys were commanded to commit rape and murder; girls, some just entering puberty, were hauled into the bush, turned into sex slaves, and impregnated by much older men. Lips that spoke out of turn were padlocked or sliced off. Earlobes and noses were ripped away, and hands were chopped at the wrist with the blade of a *panga*, a long, sharp machete. Abductees who tried to escape or who refused to follow orders to kill their own family members were shot down.

Civilians who happened to break past the barriers set up by the Ugandan military were at risk of being hijacked along the highway, even near the popular tourist destination of Karuma Falls, where natural rock formations cause rippling waters to foam like the ocean. Out of nowhere, bullets would fly, buses would burn and startled passengers would be robbed, raped or abducted—or all three. Such human rights atrocities differed greatly from those seen during the African slave trade, where men captured men, choosing the strongest to sell at auction or carry the backbreaking goods as if they were no more than mules. Kony's soldiers were not so selective.

Sister Rosemary's first brush with the violence had come just after volunteers from a British non-governmental organization (NGO), procured by Father Luigi to drive her from Moyo to Gulu, dropped her off at her new home at the Sacred Heart Secondary School. On the way back, rebels ambushed the volunteers' vehicle, abducted them and drove them to Sudan. Rosemary never knew what became of them, but it would be a long time before she could travel that road, now blocked by military officers trying to catch the insurgents.

Situated at the strategic intersection of the Victoria Nile, Albert Nile and River Achwa, Gulu served as the commercial epicenter of northern Uganda during British colonization and was still the largest city in the region despite the ensuing war and the poverty that now gripped much of the area. Thick savannah grass and other vegetation covered much of the surrounding district and offered a natural haven for wildlife.

The Sacred Heart School had been founded by a group of Italian nuns and later passed on to an African congregation called Mary Immaculate, whose Sisters were known for their forward-thinking approach to the advancement of women in many fields. A number of female doctors, lawyers and other professionals holding important positions in Uganda received their higher education here, as did nuns who felt a calling to serve their communities as nurses and medics.

Rosemary and three other Sisters lived in a long house a few meters away from the school compound but very near the main road, with no protection. On one side were small rooms for meetings between two or three people; on the other were a chapel, a little parlor and a dining room. Sister Rosemary and the other nuns slept in small bedrooms at the end of the hallway. More buildings housed the kitchen and classrooms, while a tiny garden provided vegetables, and banana and mango trees offered a bit of shade as well as sweet fruit for meals.

Assigned to her usual leadership role, she was responsible for maintaining the house, overseeing the Sisters, and offering spiritual and physical sustenance to the local residents when needed.

Despite the turmoil surrounding the school—it was not uncommon for Kony's terrorist soldiers to storm into a classroom, scattering the women and sending them scurrying under tables and desks, or rush into the chapel and disrupt the parishioners during worship service—Sister Rosemary kept attending daytime classes in her quest to become a paramedic. It was difficult to concentrate, and she was afraid, but she had to stay strong for the sake of the others.

Some days, she and the other Sisters were compelled to stay inside the house, reading books in the double-walled corridor, where bullets were unlikely to enter, and even cooking their meals there. At night, they slept on the floor, huddled together by 5:00 in the evening as a safety precaution against stray shots that might pierce the building's four large windows, most of which were now shattered by gunfire.

After a while, the Sisters grew accustomed to being afraid. Hour after hour, as bombs exploded nearby and rebels broke into their house, pilfering money and medicine and mattresses, their hearts raced at the thought of what might happen next. Once, as the terrorists charged into the compound, Sister Rosemary hid the people who ran into their house for refuge under the altar and waited with them for the room to grow silent. Another time, the four Sisters crouched low in one bathroom, screaming so loudly when the soldiers opened the door that the men threw up their hands and left. The rebels, however, were never far away, their voices penetrating the walls as they passed by in the street.

Realizing they were spending much of their time locked in fear, one day Sister Rosemary told the other Sisters, "Let us do a bit of work to get our minds on something else." Mixing a paste of masonry cement and water, the nuns built a low brick wall to serve as a buffer against flooding in the rainy season. "Even if we can't study," Sister Rosemary said, her hands on her hips, "we can do something useful here that will always remain."

Most days, it was too risky to leave the compound, with military roadblocks restricting the nuns' ability to drive to the town center for supplies. Even if they made it there safely, it was difficult to distinguish the rebels from the Ugandan soldiers. Sometimes the terrorists dressed in government uniforms stolen from the Army, sometimes in street clothes, so it was hard to tell the good guys from the bad. The only way to know for sure was by observing their attacks on the villagers, but even then, as the Ugandan militia tried to subdue them, they were apt to dart among the civilians, peel off their uniforms and disappear into the crowd.

Unlike Sister Alice, a Madi native, and Devota, a Lugbara, neither of whom understood the local Acholi dialect, Rosemary did, as did Lily Grace, who also hailed from the Alur tribe and spoke almost the same language. This came as some small comfort since the rebel soldiers considered "outsiders" their enemies and deserving targets of their violence.

Sister Rosemary held one more advantage, one that frightened her greatly at first. Some of the soldiers she had treated while running the clinic in Moyo, tending their wounds, delivering their wives' babies and conducting pre-natal classes in the barracks, had defected to the LRA. And they knew her by name.

Her ability to identify the insurgents if the Ugandan soldiers interrogated her could prove to be very dangerous. If the rebels found out she had revealed anything about them— what they looked like, what they were wearing, what direction they turned when they left the Sacred Heart campus—they would likely kill her. *Lord, let me never come face to face with these rebels*, she prayed. *If by chance I do, help them to see Your face in me so they will not harm me. And help me to see Your face in them so that I do and say the right thing.*

Eventually, she and the other nuns mustered the courage to walk to town for supplies. A lump rose in Sister Rosemary's throat when she saw the group of men headed their way, rebels returning from an attack in a nearby village.

One of the soldiers pointed to her, and she recognized him as a former officer of the Ugandan Army. "That is Rosemary," Apau told his comrades. Sister Rosemary was close enough to hear him, and his words made her heart race. What would they do to her? Would they let her pass? What should she say?

"How do you know her?" asked one of his companions.

"She is our doctor."

Apau, now an LRA commander, then spoke directly to Sister Rosemary. "Are you here in Gulu now?"

"Yes, I am." Sister Rosemary smiled, nodded and kept walking. The rebels did nothing to stop her or the other nuns.

Later that evening, Apau appeared on her doorstep. "Sister, the next time we are going to attack, I will let you know. Stay in the house and do not go outside. You will be safe."

Apau kept his word, warning Sister Rosemary of impending danger not once, but twice. Sometimes she and the other Sisters marveled at how they managed to stay alive.

Not all of the rebels knew her, however, nor did they show mercy. One night, while Sister Rosemary was on business in Kampala, a group of insurgents attacked the nuns' house, chipping away at the concrete door with a machete until, two hours later, they managed to break inside.

Fearing for their lives, the other Sisters hid in the bathroom, listening in silence as the rebels rummaged through their things, stealing food, personal belongings—including the radio in Sister Rosemary's room—and the little money they had.

As soon as Sister Alice called to tell her what had happened, Rosemary left Kampala and returned to Gulu to be with the other Sisters. She could not let them suffer this hardship alone.

One of the most serious attacks came in the middle of the afternoon, with sudden gunfire exchanged between rebel and Ugandan soldiers prompting strangers to run for cover inside the house where Sister Rosemary and the other Sisters lived. Desperate to find a safe place, perhaps one where a Godly presence would shield them from harm, the people hid in the chapel, in the small meeting areas, in the nuns' private rooms.

More than three hours had passed since the gunshots began, stray bullets pelting the exterior of the house. Sister Rosemary could no longer hear any noise rising from the street, and she was growing restless to feed the hungry people who were depending on her.

"I'm going to open the door and see if anything is happening outside or if I can see any people moving," she told the Sisters who had been huddling together, silent and still. "Maybe we can cook something for ourselves now."

"No, don't go!" the other nuns pleaded. "What if they're waiting for you?"

The Sisters might be right, but Rosemary couldn't just sit here all day and night, hungry and afraid. She had to do something. "I'll be fine. We can't remain here like this. I need to find out."

Standing tall, Sister Rosemary made her way to the small, crude kitchen in the next building. As she drew near, she noticed something that made her catch her breath. The door was half open now, but it had been closed when the gunfire began. She had made sure of that. Bracing herself, she stepped into the room just as the rebel emerged from behind the door.

It took all the courage she could muster to calmly face the soldier and squash the urge to escape. "What are you doing here? What do you want?" she asked in the man's native *Acholi.*

"Sister, my gun could not work anymore. It's stuck," he told her. "The government soldiers are passing nearby, and they will catch me here, unarmed. My comrades have gone and I want to leave too, but I have no working gun, and I'm hungry. Do you have any food?"

When faced with someone stronger and more aggressive, Sister Rosemary had learned to suppress the temptation to become aggressive herself, to box the bullies as she had in grade school. Her weapon, instead, was kindness, her shield a prayer of surrender: *God, please let me see the face of Jesus in anyone who comes to me, even someone with a bad heart. And let that person see the face of Jesus in me.* Confronting another person out of anger or fear would only make matters worse and cause them to attack, like a startled lion prodded with a stick. In dangerous situations, vulnerability became her strength, and her "weakness" disarmed the strong.

Sister Rosemary retrieved a small sack of groundnuts, scooped up a handful and dropped them in the rebel's pocket, along with a couple of potatoes.

"Thank you," he said. "Do you have any medicine?"

"Yes. What do you need?"

"Something for pain."

Sister Rosemary exited the room and returned with two plastic bottles, one filled with aspirin, another with Panadol. She handed both to the rebel just as a curious Sister Alice peeked in the kitchen to see whom Rosemary was talking to.

"You must go away now," Sister Rosemary told the young man. "If the Ugandan soldiers find me helping you, we will all be in trouble. They will kill all of us."

The soldier picked up his useless gun and, with Sister Rosemary accompanying him part of the way, ran to the other side of the road. The Sacred Heart compound had become a popular passageway for all types of people—rebels, government soldiers, parishioners—so she was anxious for him to be gone lest he encounter the authorities and blurt out the details of their conversation.

Then, to Rosemary's dismay, the young man turned and ran back to the room where he had been hiding. "Sister, I can't leave you in trouble like this."

Bewildered, she followed him, unable to fathom what could be so important that he would risk his own life, and hers, by delaying his escape. Inside the kitchen, he opened the door of the white wood-fired oven and began to pluck bullets from the ashes left behind from the last meal. "Before you came in, I put these in your oven," he said, furiously plucking the projectile weapons from the spots where he had hidden them—not just the oven, but from the flour, made of dried cassava and millet, set out for the day's bread-making. "You have been good to me. I can't leave them here to blow up in your face."

By the time the rebel soldier had finished removing the bullets, Sister Rosemary realized he had concealed enough of them to explode the entire house when she and the Sisters cooked dinner that night.

In 1988, two years after arriving at the Sacred Heart Secondary School, Rosemary gave up her classes, for it had become just too difficult to continue. Elected Superior of her congregation, she began studying on her own, eventually completing her studies through private tutoring and passing all of her exams.

But the insurgency was far from over, and the reign of terror continued to create extreme hardship for the Sisters. Frightened neighbors often ran to their house during attacks, seeking refuge. When two of the school's future medical students moved in with the nuns, Sister Rosemary dressed them in veils and habits to shield them from harm. "Girls, I'm not trying to get you to become Sisters," she joked. "I'm trying to protect you."

This would not be the last time Sister Rosemary camouflaged someone with the sacred uniform intended solely for those who have taken their vows.

As the violence raged on in Gulu, friends kept urging Catherine Okech and her husband Stephen to leave their house and take refuge at the hospital nearby.

"No, we will stay," Stephen said. "If we have a problem, the dogs will growl and let us know."

It was late afternoon when Catherine returned from driving her older children back to the boarding school. She knew the routine: Be home before sunset, cook and eat the last meal of the day long before dark, and go to bed early. By 7:00 in the evening, the roads would be deserted, no cars in sight.

Stephen had just finished bathing and was getting dressed when his wife called out to him.

"What? What's the problem?"

"There are people outside." Catherine had never seen them before.

"Stay away from the window!" By the time Stephen emerged from the bedroom, the intruders were already banging on the door of the adjacent house, where Stephen's mother lived.

"Don't go, Daddy!" his daughter pleaded. "They will kill you!"

Stephen said nothing, but left the room for a moment and returned with his shotgun, intent on rescuing his mother. He was a religious man but he was also a retired military officer, and he must protect his family at all costs.

But his terrified daughter wasn't about to cave in. "Daddy, if you go out, I'll follow you!"

Stephen sighed and took a step back. As much as he feared for his mother, he couldn't risk losing his daughter, and he had no way to stop her from coming after him if she was determined to do so.

Switching off the lights, he motioned for Catherine and the other children to line up quietly against the wall so no one could peer at them through the window.

"There's a boy in the house!" one of the rebels shouted outside. "Let's go get him."

"Children, don't move," Stephen said. "The Lord will guide us."

With his right index finger resting lightly on the trigger, Stephen lunged through the front door and shot the man in the neck. The other soldiers ran, dropping the children's bicycles and the rest of the things they had gathered. Stephen picked up the dead man's gun, brought it inside and closed the door.

The phone lines were dead, so there was no way to call the police. The couple stayed up all night and, early the next morning, a Sunday, Stephen paid a visit to the Bishop, then the authorities, and told them what had happened. Before he left, he instructed his family to dress in their church clothes; they would be safe at the Sacred Heart mission.

Catherine and the children managed to walk to the chapel unharmed. Suddenly, her relief gave way to panic. "There she is! That is the woman we are looking for!" It was one of the rebels who had been at her house the day before.

Catherine had even more reason than most to fear for her life; she was originally from Mbarara, the hometown of President Museveni, and that made her both a foreigner and an enemy of the LRA. Easily winded from the weight she had gained over the years, she walked quickly with no thought to where she was going. Sister Rosemary looked up from her breakfast, startled, as the barefoot, frightened woman burst into the dining room.

"Catherine! What's wrong?"

"Sister, last night the rebels attacked our home and my husband killed one of them in self-defense. Now they are chasing me. Please, can we stay here with you? I want to go back to our house and get our things."

"Of course." Rosemary took off her flip-flops and handed them to the woman. "Here, put these on. You can walk faster."

Back on the street, Catherine whipped around a corner and nearly ran into the two rebels, their pistols drawn. Turning on her heel and running back to the nuns' house, this time she didn't stop until she had reached Sister Rosemary's small room and wiggled her bulging body under the bed.

Locking the front door behind her, Sister Rosemary soon heard one of the students pleading outside. "Sisters, please open the door! Open the door for me. Please!"

As Sister Rosemary unlocked the bolt, the rebels released their grip on the girl and stormed into the house. "Where is the lady who ran here?" they demanded. "Tell us if this woman is here!"

"We saw someone pass by but we don't know where she went," Rosemary and her Sisters lied. "No one is here but us."

"Tell us or we'll kill you!"

Jesus, protect us. Protect us from harm, Rosemary prayed, clutching the ivory cross she wore around her neck every day, a gift from Father Luigi.

Under the bed, Catherine was breathing so loudly she was sure her pursuers would hear. Through the hem of the thin quilt, she could see the feet of a rebel soldier pacing around in the room.

"She's not here!" he shouted to his comrade. "Let us leave these stupid people alone."

Slamming the door, the soldier looked over his shoulder at Sister Rosemary. "We'll be back!"

As soon as they were gone, Catherine began to weep.

"Catherine, don't cry," Sister Rosemary said, bending down to look under the bed before helping the woman to her feet, no easy task for a petite nun barely five-foot-one-inch tall. "Don't cry. Keep praying. God will take care of you."

Catherine wiped the tears from her eyes. "What about tonight? Those men will come back for me. Sister, I am so afraid. What do I do?"

Sister Rosemary pondered the situation. "I'll think of something."

But what? If the rebels saw the woman leaving the house, they would know Sister Rosemary had lied and would never trust her again. They might even kill them both.

Maybe she could dress her in one of the nuns' habits. But how? Catherine was huge, and none of their uniforms would fit her.

Then, quite by instinct—or perhaps it was divine guidance—Sister Rosemary walked to another room, unlatched a seldom-used wooden wardrobe, and began rifling through the garments. Tucked between other articles of clothing was a worn, dusty dress that had once belonged to a plus-size Sister who no longer lived at the compound, and a veil.

Shaking out the old uniform, she handed it to Catherine. "Here, put this on."

Trembling with fear that the rebels would come back and catch them, and fervently praying for the safety of everyone in the house, the other nuns gathered around Catherine, quickly dressing her in the borrowed garb like teens nervously helping a friend prepare for an impromptu date.

As evening fell, Sister Rosemary and the other nuns accompanied Catherine past the Mary Immaculate convent, to a pickup truck belonging to Sisters from that congregation.

"Don't cry," they told Catherine, whose eyes were swollen from all the tears she had shed. "If you cry, they are going to know who you are. Just behave as if you are one of us."

Two of the Mary Immaculate Sisters sandwiched Catherine between them, shrouding her terrified face with the veil, and another, Sister Palma, climbed into the driver's seat. Sister Rosemary stood guard outside the door. The two rebels happened to walk by the house just as the vehicle pulled away. "Make sure you catch that woman!" their commander shouted to Rosemary. "Make sure you catch her!"

Years would pass before Sister Rosemary would know what happened to the friend she had smuggled out of the compound, but she knew in her soul that God had saved Catherine.

The getaway nuns prayed hard as they neared the corner where government officers were stationed, checking each vehicle for insurgents.

"Sister Palma, where are you going?" an officer asked when the pickup came to a stop.

"We are going to pray in town and will be back in one hour. Only one hour."

The man glanced into the truck, then nodded. "All right. Proceed."

The Sisters arrived at a Catholic diocese house, where Catherine remained in her fake uniform until it was time for her benefactors to take her to a local hospital. There, the "sick" woman was loaded into an ambulance and transported to Kampala, where she would be safe.

Years later, when Sister Rosemary saw her again, Catherine asserted, "If it weren't for you, I would not be alive today." The two women remained close, and as they grew up, Catherine's children would sometimes ask to hear the story of how a little Catholic nun saved their mother's life.

By 1989 the brutal conditions in Gulu had become too much for the Sisters to bear, so Rosemary came up with a scheme to help them return to the Mother House in Moyo. If they moved all their belongings with them, they would draw attention to themselves and risk a violent attack from the insurgents. But with looting so common, they could not leave their things—tables and chairs, cups and saucers, blankets and pillows—behind. Their congregation was so small, and so poor, that it would be nearly impossible to replace the stolen items in the future. Even if they were killed trying to escape, the nuns who lived here next would need these things.

Sister Rosemary had an idea. "Okay, ladies, this is what we're going to do," she instructed. Pacing themselves so as not to alert the rebels to what they were doing, they began squirreling away supplies and storing them in a small, rarely used room of the house. Piece by piece, the other Sisters handed them up to Rosemary, who stood on a balcony above them, carefully tucking the items into the hiding place.

When they were finished, the four Sisters locked the door behind them and, in one day's time, covered it up with plaster and bricks. Then they painted it the same color as the rest of the wall and shoved a large, freestanding cupboard against it.

After making their way to a house in Gulu, one of a sparse group of buildings known as Saint Monica Girls' Tailoring Centre, they waited for seven days, with no food, for the military escort that would take them back to the West Nile. The journey there normally took one day, but it took a whole week, and a detour west to Arua, for the convoy to transport the four Sisters and the other fleeing passengers all the way to Moyo.

Delivered safely to the Mother House, Sister Rosemary soon felt the effects of what some might call post-traumatic stress disorder. Darkness terrified her, and she jumped at the slightest noise. She constantly locked doors behind her. Marveling at the sight of people milling about the property long past 5:00 in the evening—the Sisters' self-imposed curfew in Gulu—she found it difficult to relax and adjust to feeling safe again.

Having proven her leadership skills, Rosemary was appointed Provincial Superior over all the Sacred Heart Sisters in Uganda and Kenya. Barely thirty years old, at first she didn't feel ready, but her longtime confidante, Father Luigi, pushed her to accept the post. With it came much responsibility, which she accepted with her usual grace and positive attitude. She quickly earned the respect of her underlings and, at a time when Catholic nuns in other parts of Africa were forsaking their vows and leaving their congregations, saw a very low turnover rate in her own. Her elders and the priests with whom she worked often credited this success to her patient nature and genuine appreciation for other people. She was never afraid to try something new, to buck the religious trends or the culture, to speak her mind in a tactful, convincing way. Building relationships was always a priority for Sister Rosemary, whose strong listening skills and intuitive sense led her to take other opinions and ideas seriously rather than dismiss them.

Never complacent about her own education, when her leadership office ended she resumed her studies at a senior secondary school, Trinity College, in Kampala, and two years later received her "A" level certification. After that, she attended Uganda Martyrs University in Nkozi, fifty miles west of Kampala, where she earned an undergraduate degree in development studies and ethics. Martyrs University then offered her a scholarship, allowing her to earn a master's degree in the same field.

Despite the demands of her classes and her administrative duties at the Moyo convent and surrounding communities, Sister Rosemary set aside time to visit other facilities, including Saint Monica Girls' Tailoring Centre, where she and the other Sisters had hidden after escaping from their besieged house in Gulu. It was at St. Monica's, while meeting with her friend Father Donald Dunson, an American theologian and the founder of the St. Kizito Foundation serving vulnerable children in Uganda, that her courage was once again tested.

Sister Rosemary and Father Dunson had just finished Sunday morning Mass and sat down to eat breakfast when they heard students shouting at the back of the house near the chicken coop. Racing outside, they spotted a large cobra, head raised, neck fanned, ready to attack a squawking hen, who was frantically trying to cover her eggs. The high-pitched screams of the students and the other Sisters only made the snake more aggressive.

Rosemary inched closer to the beast. She had to do something to save the hen and, more importantly, the students at the compound. On the loose, the deadly snake could pose a grave danger to the girls living there. Even if it did not kill its prey, it could spit venom into the victim's eyes, rendering it blind.

"No Sister, stop!" yelled one of the nuns. "I'll go get help!"

As Rosemary stood guard near the hooded creature, the other Sister darted outside and waved down a passing "Boda Boda Man." Known for screeching their loud motorbike taxis through traffic jams and dangerous terrain to transport passengers across national borders without the paperwork required of cars and trucks, the boda-boda drivers had developed a reputation as tough and defiant. Once inside the chicken coop, however, the man took one look at the cobra and ran.

Sister Rosemary had no choice but to take matters into her own hands. Seizing a garden rake with a long handle, she lifted the implement high and brought it down hard on the cobra's head. The second blow left it quiet and motionless on the floor.

For Sister Rosemary, the snakes she had fought in her life—the one that bit her in the dark when she was a novice, the menacing beast in the ceiling of the orphanage store, the cobra in the chicken house—had become symbols of hardship and challenge. If one person could save others from imminent danger, it was well worth the risk, and she was no stranger to risk-taking.

Back in Moyo, Sister Rosemary faced other dangers as she ministered to refugees driven from their homes by the LRA terrorists. Living in squalor in Internally Displaced Persons (IDP) camps, where the Ugandan government had ordered them to move to protect them from the rebel soldiers, they shared tiny, grass-roofed mud houses built so close together that if one caught fire, the others would too. Sanitation was extremely poor, with no clean water and no privacy, and disease and violence were rampant. For the nearly two million IDPs who lived in the crowded camps at the height of the terrorist crisis, there was no way to make a living and little chance of maintaining one's dignity and pride.

Sister Rosemary frequently traveled to one of the IDP encampments with Sister Alice Kinyaa to offer spiritual care to the refugees from Sudan and northern Uganda.

It was dark when the two women arrived at the camp in Adjumani, this time to carry out a research project for an academic paper. A handful of priests and a few other Sisters who were there to provide medical and personal care for the refugees sat outside the nuns' one-room hut, taking a break.

Road-weary and in dire need of a bath, Sister Rosemary and Sister Alice excused themselves from the group, walked to the public bathing area and cleaned up for the night. Moments after rejoining the others, Rosemary felt the barrel of a gun pressed to her back.

"You are enjoying life." Muttered in Swahili, the phrase was a strange one, even for a terrorist.

Sister Rosemary turned to glance at the gunman, then ran around the house in her nightdress, a towel still wrapped around her head, and hid in the bushes nearby. Miraculously, the assailant did not pursue her, choosing instead to round up the other Sisters in the small house and lock them inside. The priests bolted for the safety of their own hut.

"Give me everything you have in this place, and do not look up," the rebel ordered. "Keep your face down."

"We have no money," the Sisters protested. "We don't have anything."

But the man was not about to give up. Rummaging through the nuns' belongings, he found a few shillings donated by the church and stuffed them into his pocket.

Suddenly, one of the Fathers, who had awakened from a nap in the priests' hut nearby, jumped in his car and drove toward the house, foot pressed hard on the accelerator, headlights glaring, in an effort to scare off the gunman. Hearing the sound of the engine, the rebel stepped outside, locked the door behind him and aimed his gun at the priest. From behind a clump of shrubs, Sister Rosemary watched the clergyman clutch his wounded, bleeding hand before the insurgent threw open the car door and dragged him into the house.

"If you don't give me what I ask, you will all be like this," the soldier warned as blood poured from his victim's hand.

Selecting one Sister to move with him and carry the random items he had stolen, the gunman headed straight for the spot where Rosemary was hiding. If she stayed there, he would surely catch her. So in the dead of night, wearing only a nightgown, she ran as fast as she could, leaping over thick knots of grass like a wild animal fleeing from a predator.

"Please open the door!" she begged, pounding on the entrance to a hut where one of the refugees lived. "I am Sister Rosemary and we are being attacked! Please open the door! Somebody's following me!"

A man appeared in the doorway, and the breathless nun rushed inside. "We heard gunshots," he said. "But we didn't know the Sisters were involved."

"Yes, and I can't go back there right now."

All night, Rosemary stayed in the family's hut, never sleeping, and at 6:00 in the morning she walked back toward the house of the Sisters.

"Rosemary, where have you been?" they exclaimed. "We worried so much about you. We thought you were killed. Thank goodness you are safe!"

Except for the priest's hand, the gunman had inflicted no physical injuries. The incident, however, brought back painful memories for Sister Rosemary, memories that disrupted her sleep and plagued her waking thoughts with dread.

For a while, life was calmer, with few incidents of violence marring the peaceful environment in Moyo. Then in 2001, her Superiors announced, "Rosemary, we are sorry because we know you had many problems there, but we're asking you to go back to Gulu."

For a moment, anxiety clouded Sister Rosemary's heart. Then she remembered her calling: to minister to those in need, wherever they needed her. "Don't apologize. I will go wherever you send me. If I am supposed to be in Gulu, I will build a life even on top of water."

She had hoped that the past was finally behind her—all the trauma, the terror, the uncertainty. But God had other plans.

PART TWO

CHAPTER SIX

HIDDEN HORROR

St. Monica's Girls' School in Gulu, Uganda

Despite the deceptively lush vegetation flanking the entrance to the school grounds, Saint Monica Girls' Tailoring Centre was almost abandoned. A large banyan tree towered at one end of the compound, its leathery leaves offering shade from the tropical sun, its thick trunk forked in a tangle of prop roots like wooden stalagmites rising from the earth. Mangos, avocados and lemons flourished near bushy tamarinds bearing mature, sweet pods, while pink bougainvillea and tea roses offered bright splashes of color among succulent, gray-green aloe vera.

Metal bars on the windows echoed the spikes of the sturdy iron gate, making the campus look more like a prison than a school, and most of the doors were locked tight. The U-shaped cluster of rundown, cream-hued buildings, which could accommodate 300 people, was largely unused except for two stark rooms where fewer than thirty female students attended academic classes in tailoring and other subjects. A few spoke broken English, while only one of the two Sacred Heart Sisters, who taught a tailoring class without any official training in the subject, knew a handful of words in the girls' native Acholi. There was almost no way to gauge the students' success, and even more difficult to know much about whom they were or where they came from.

The conservative northern region of Uganda is primarily Catholic, with portraits of Jesus and the Virgin Mary hanging in many homes, and Sunday Mass the week's most important worship and social event. In 1983, a group of Comboni Italian Missionary Sisters founded a vocational training center and boarding school in Gulu. It would later be named after Saint Monica, an African-born patron saint of married women and mothers who was known for her patience with an abusive husband, ornery mother-in-law and wayward son, all of whom eventually converted to Monica's beloved Christianity.

In its early days, the center was known as Adel School in honor of Sister Adeliana, who ran it at that time, and was mostly intended to provide the uneducated women of northern Uganda with practical home economics skills to help them be better housewives. Some of the modest buildings were still under construction when members of the Lord's Resistance Army began attacking Gulu civilians in the mid-1980s. More than once, the rebels broke in, looted the place, and damaged classrooms. One nun was shot in the finger, which had to be amputated.

In 2000, the Comboni Sisters handed over the management of St. Monica's to the Archdiocese of Gulu, who in turn entrusted it to a group of Sisters of the Sacred Heart of Jesus who had fled the unbearable war conditions in south Sudan. The Sacred Heart Sisters, however, were given little direction about their responsibilities at the school, which by now was nearly in shambles, just like everything else Joseph Kony had left in his path of destruction.

When Sister Rosemary arrived a year later, the school was grossly underutilized and running at a heavy financial loss. Despite the establishment of St. Monica's as a school for women from all parts of northern Uganda, tribal conflicts had prevented those outside the village from attending. Guerrilla soldiers were terrorizing the region, murdering adults and abducting hundreds of children for indoctrination into Kony's army. Compounding these problems, an Ebola outbreak was sweeping Gulu, and the virus had already claimed many lives.

No one, not even the Bishop, knew what to do with the place. But one thing was certain: If anyone could come up with a plan, even under these desperate circumstances, it was Sister

Rosemary Nyirumbe. She had proven herself to be strong, energetic and capable, with a knack for seeing the possible within the impossible. Her new mission, her superiors said behind closed doors, *must* be successful. She was the only one who could salvage St. Monica's. She could not fail.

Sister Rosemary hadn't a clue how to revive the nearly dead school. She was neither a teacher nor a tailor, but she *was* a trained midwife with a degree in development studies, so she decided to use her sharp listening skills and powers of observation to find out more about the girls and how to connect with them. At least she knew Acholi, which enabled her to break through the language barrier and communicate with the students, and that was a start. *I'm not trained to run a school like this*, she thought to herself. *But I will behave like I can.*

Among the students at St. Monica's was a girl who would never look anyone else in the eye. She seemed frightened and sad all the time and often flinched when spoken to.

"Jewel, will you come with me?" Sister Rosemary asked one day, leading the girl into her office. "I want to speak with you."

Jewel obediently followed the nun, never lifting her gaze.

"Why don't you ever look at anyone?" Sister Rosemary gently asked. "What's wrong?"

Jewel responded by staring even more intently at the floor and clasping her hands in her lap.

"Can you look at me?"

The girl fixed her gaze on the wall, as if distracted by some mystical object in the distance.

Sister Rosemary decided to try a different approach. "Jewel, am I so ugly that you cannot look at me?"

A soft chuckle escaped from Jewel's lips. "No, Sister Rosemary, you're not ugly."

"Then look at me. Look right into my eyes if I am not ugly."

The girl lifted her chin and glanced in Sister Rose's direction.

"Jewel, why do you always keep to yourself? You don't talk to your teachers or the other girls in class."

"Sister, my eyes are always in pain."

Rosemary could see nothing wrong with the girl's eyes. "Why are they hurting?"

Jewel took a deep breath. Then, in a faltering voice, she explained why it was so difficult for her to study with the other students.

"Sister," she said, "I was with the rebels for nine years, and I was a commanding officer, always taking the front line. I helped them kill many people, and the smoke from the gunshots affected my eyesight."

It had never occurred to Sister Rosemary that one of the girls at St. Monica's might be a former abductee of the LRA regime or that she might have participated in barbarism against her own people. *Dear Jesus,* she prayed. *Please help me know what to say.*

It was difficult for Jewel to speak about her past, something she seldom did. She had been snatched from her family as a child and, against her will, trained as a rebel soldier. Forced to live in the bush with other captives, she emerged only to attack the villagers, steal from them and kill those who put up a fight or got in her way.

"I'm afraid the other girls will find out what I did, who I was," she said. "They will not understand. They will talk about me behind my back and be suspicious of everything I do.

"Sister, I can't keep up in the dress-making class," she added. "The rebels kidnapped me while I was still in school, and I never learned how to do the math and other things I am expected to do."

Listening to Jewel's heart-wrenching story, Sister Rosemary realized that the girl, and others like her, had lost not just their homes, their innocence and their self-esteem, but because they had been deprived of school at an early age, a basic education. How could someone like that possibly master a sewing curriculum that required students to calculate how much fabric to cut without actually cutting the fabric?

Then she had an idea.

"Jewel, what do you think about me starting a practical tailoring class, where you would learn to sew dresses and not just study from books?"

The girl nodded, slowly at first, then with more conviction. "I will try."

CHAPTER SEVEN

A NEW MISSION

Young girls learning practical skills

By 2002, Sister Rosemary had, through her own powers of persuasion, secured funding to purchase several foot-pedal Singer sewing machines and start the first hands-on class at Saint Monica Girls' Tailoring Centre. To her surprise, ten of the thirty students signed up. All ten, she later learned, had escaped from Joseph Kony's army.

Using only a tape measure and a pair of shears, and without the aid of printed patterns or dressmaking models, each girl learned to estimate how much fabric she needed for a particular garment, and how to cut it. Repeatedly pumping their worn, unlaced shoes on the wide foot pedals of the old-fashioned black machines, the tailoring students sewed dresses and blouses and undergarments, and sometimes embellished the pieces with decorative embroidery and beautiful crocheted stitches. Sister Rosemary deliberately steered away from the theoretical, scientific lessons that had previously been taught at St. Monica's and focused instead on practical skills the young women could take with them when they graduated.

"Sister, can we join the class too?" asked other girls when they heard about the tailoring lessons.

"No, the class has already begun. You'll have to wait till next time."

Sister Rosemary made a point to encourage the tailoring pupils, especially Jewel, who quickly grasped her lessons and produced quality garments with perfect collars, cuffs and buttonholes.

"Jewel, I am going to the market to do some shopping," Sister Rosemary said one day. "Would you like to come with me?"

Before long, the girl was accompanying Sister Rosemary on a regular basis. "Okay, I'm going this way. You go that way and pick up some corn and millet," the nun would say, handing Jewel enough Ugandan shillings to pay for the purchase, plus a few more. "Then we'll meet at the car." Jewel seemed puzzled at first that someone would trust her. Most of the people in her village now viewed her with suspicion, as if, at any moment, she might resort to her previous rebel activities and harm them.

Little by little, she began to look other people in the eye and speak more directly to them. She even grew accustomed to being in public again, and often assisted Sister Rosemary in the kitchen. To Jewel's amazement, someone was singling her out not for the horrible acts she had committed in the past, but for the positive things she could do now.

At the end of the school year, Jewel passed the first practical tailoring class with distinction, by far the best seamstress in her group.

Sister Rosemary's initial fear of returning to Gulu had given way to hope, and she vowed to help more girls like Jewel.

"This war has affected our students more than we ever imagined," she told the other Sisters. "These girls need other practical skills to make up for the lessons they missed while they were living in captivity. We can do more than just dressmaking and cutting."

Before long she had added a cooking class and taught the girls how to bake unique dishes, from heart-shaped lemon cakes to cabbage casserole with eggs, and how to squeeze sweet mango juice from the green fruit. Gradually, Sister Rosemary introduced ethnic cuisine from the Sudanese and Italian nuns with whom she had worked, and showed the students how to decorate cakes for special occasions. Over time, business professionals in Gulu heard about the extraordinary culinary skills of the girls at St. Monica's and began to inquire about their availability to cater public events.

"Will you help me find a driver?" Rosemary's older sister Catherine, now a state minister of public service, asked one day. "I've been invited to Gulu for a conference and I need someone to drive me around all week."

Rosemary had the perfect solution. "I'll do it."

By now she was adept at spotting opportunities to fund her students' projects. What's more, she had access to a dependable pickup and, unlike many of her colleagues, knew how to drive. An Italian Brother had taught her when, upon arriving at the primitive clinic in Moyo, the twenty-five-year-old Sister stubbornly insisted on being able to rush emergency patients to the hospital herself. To a group of local boys who wanted to learn after that, Brother Gusma had joked, "I will only teach you if you can put the car in reverse as well as Sister Rosemary."

With the money she earned from her stint as Catherine's driver—the fee was equivalent to 100 American dollars—she paid a handful of Gulu residents to clear the compound of rubbish and remove unsightly stumps to make the property more presentable to visitors. But there was another hurdle: Where would the Sisters find the catering equipment and food supplies they needed in order to host public events at the school?

"I'll pay you back in one month," Sister Rosemary told a shop owner in Gulu, explaining the situation. "Please let me take these things on credit so we can get started." Such a bold statement was risky, she knew. It could even land her in prison if she failed to keep her word. But few people could refuse the little nun with the big heart, especially when her mind was made up, and before long the shop floor was piled high with food items, serving plates, and dishes fit for a royal banquet.

Back at St. Monica's, she unloaded the supplies, sat down with pen and paper, and wrote her first radio announcement: *Saint Monica Girls' Training Centre is now offering catering and rental space for parties, conferences and meetings. Please call the school to schedule an event.*

"Which Sister is talking so much on the radio?" a school inspector wanted to know, peeking his head in her office soon after the announcements started airing.

Rosemary smiled broadly. "That is me."

"Are you sure you can run a catering service?"

"Absolutely," Sister Rosemary said, undeterred.

The man grinned. "Can you handle a large group of teachers?"

"How many?"

"A lot."

The teachers' conference—the first of many catering gigs at St. Monica's—paid approximately 5,000 American dollars. Sister Rosemary was able to pay off the 3,000 dollars she had charged and squirrel away the profits for the next event. Demand quickly grew as the school hosted more and more conferences, seminars, wedding receptions, graduation ceremonies and meetings. And the villagers, who had kept their distance from the students at St. Monica's, even from girls they had known well before the kidnappings but no longer trusted because of their past affiliation with the rebels, began hiring them as tailors and cooks.

From 8:30 in the morning until 4:00 in the afternoon, the students attended classes in sewing and catering as well as English, science and math. Because she felt it was important to their heritage and sense of belonging, Sister Rosemary also set aside time for them to practice the traditional dances of their native tribes.

Sister Rosemary's entrepreneurial spirit was stoked, and she found herself thinking of ways to raise money to keep the new programs going. There were many youngsters wearing many uniforms at many schools in northern Uganda and southern Sudan, and *someone* had to make them. Why not the experienced tailoring students at St. Monica's? Within weeks, she had set up a new production section in tailoring class, allowing the girls to generate revenue by sewing uniforms for other schools in the region.

As usual, Sister Rosemary implemented the new classes and generally relied on the talents of her staff when it came to the finances and other details. As the voice of St. Monica's, she marketed the school with the fervor of a seasoned business owner.

"Let us make a radio announcement and invite all the girls who came from captivity, and their children," she told the Sisters. "We can give them the same skills that we are giving the girls who are here now."

"But what will we do with the children?" the nuns asked.

"We will take care of them. God will provide a way."

The only radio station in Gulu, Mega FM had been established by a Dutchman but was now run by the locals. Its objective was to encourage the people, even young LRA recruits who might be considering defecting from Kony's army, and motivate them with hope for a better life.

Sister Rosemary wrote a short script and delivered it to the station for the deejay to read. "We know there are girls out there who are interested in learning practical dressmaking and cutting," the announcer stated. "St. Monica's welcomes all girls who came from captivity, all the child mothers who were forced to serve as soldiers alongside the rebels. Come as you are, with your children, or even if you are pregnant. We'll take you, no matter who you are, and give you the training you need to make a living. Registration starts in three days."

Sister Rosemary was attending to church business in Kampala when the announcement aired. Curious to see if there had been any response, she phoned Sister Teresa at the school.

"Did any new students come?"

"Oh, Sister," the nun said. "We are in trouble. There are so many girls waiting outside, and they keep coming. What do we do with them?"

Sister Rosemary returned to find dozens of young women sitting in the shade of the enormous banyan tree in the roundabout at the entrance to St. Monica's. Some tucked their hair inside turbans. Many bounced babies on their hips.

Most brought no possessions with them. Three-quarters were LRA escapees.

Painfully shy and withdrawn, the girls didn't say much when the nuns tried to talk to them. Their trauma, however, was obvious. The scars, the crooked knee joints and uneven gaits, the shattered jawbones and drooping eye sockets and missing earlobes said it all.

By the end of the year, 200 girls had enrolled in the tailoring and catering classes at St. Monica's. No one was turned away. Such a radical practice—openly welcoming former abductees and their children into a school, any school—had never happened before in Uganda.

Sister Rosemary suddenly found herself juggling a number of unforeseen, challenging roles: counselor, teacher, job coach. As a trained midwife, she was even prepared to deliver babies if she had to. It was as if all of her longtime personal interests, from cooking and sewing to driving and babysitting, had merged into a powerful force to serve others.

Even after the new students had settled into their classes, it was nearly impossible to get some of them to talk about the most mundane topics, much less what they had suffered while in captivity. It was frustrating, too, for the other Sisters, who had no idea what to do with these withdrawn, damaged girls and the children fathered by rebel soldiers not out of love, but of power and physical force.

"I think what we should do is love and accept these girls and walk with them, in their shoes," Sister Rosemary told the nuns. "Let us accept them as they are and not judge them for what they have done. We must treat them as normal people, not as people who have done terrible things. This is not just about giving them training. It is about giving them love.

"And please, let us not remind them of their past. Let none of you reach out and tell these girls that we know what they went through. When they're ready to talk to us, they will. We must listen to them without judging and earn their trust."

Sister Rosemary was right. Slowly, very slowly, the girls grew accustomed to having her near them, in the classroom, in the kitchen, on the grounds after dinner. Sometimes they would spot her sitting alone, under a shade tree, and cautiously perch on the bench next to her. Now and then, they would venture a few words, then a few more, until their tortured tales finally spilled out, unleashing a torrent of suppressed emotion.

Some of the girls had been raped in front of their families before being kidnapped and dragged into the bush. Others were abducted without sexual violence but later brought back to their homes to kill their own parents, siblings or other relatives. All were used as sex slaves and trained as rebel soldiers, forced to do Kony's bidding or be executed on the spot. Those who had tried to escape were shot in the leg, or their arms had been chopped off or their faces maimed. Many had watched another girl die while attempting to run. Somehow, perhaps through the same divine providence that bolstered Sister Rose and the other nuns in times of crisis, they had managed to get away in the end.

Their stories, even for someone like Sister Rosemary, who had witnessed much pain and hardship in her ministry, were horrendous. It was a heavy burden to bear. *Jesus, I don't know if I should know all these things*, she prayed in morning chapel, in Mass, in tailoring class. *Give me the strength to serve these girls, to ease their pain in some small way and give them hope. Please take care of this. It is too big for me to handle.*

With the rebel war still underway, Sister Rosemary had to fight her own fears of what might happen next. But her determination to help the girls, to restore each lost childhood, kept her from giving in to frustration and panic. Watching the students succeed in the classroom, and knowing that because of their newfound, practical skills they would never be relegated to crouching at the roadside to beg for money or food, made her as proud as if she were their real, biological mother.

Treating the former abductees just like everyone else, she would say in the years to come, had been their salvation, and hers. Here they were, all of them, African women living together and helping each other through one of northern Uganda's darkest times.

Sister Rosemary vowed never to forget what she had learned from the first group of girls who came to live at St. Monica's. "Let us make this our model for running the school," she said to the Sisters. "Let us always invite girls who have had to drop out of school, and girls who were taken into captivity, and rehabilitate them through love, care and acceptance."

One year after she arrived at St. Monica's, Sister Rosemary sat down at her desk and began typing her first formal report, one that showed far more ambition than her superiors could have imagined when they assigned her to oversee the compound.

"Training in only tailoring for three years does not provide enough opportunity for these girls and women who otherwise want other courses in life skills and problem-solving," she wrote. "For this reason, the center embarked on practical dressmaking and basic cookery for one year. These courses are offered especially to formerly abducted women. It also has become a process of continuous rehabilitation for these girls.

"We also started with seminars, workshops, graduation ceremonies, wedding celebrations and other Christian functions like meetings of different groups. The center offers catering services to the people. This was intentionally introduced to give our students a practical catering and home management experience that is very useful for them for the future."

Sister Rosemary went on to describe the new production section designed to generate operating funds and, at the same time, boost self-confidence in the girls assigned to sew uniforms for area schools. She explained how graduates of Saint Monica Girls' Tailoring Centre were being integrated back into society and gaining employment in Gulu hotels and other service-oriented establishments. Using the one-page report as a starting point, Sister Rose wrote a longer strategic plan of fifteen pages and, after preparing the final document for the Archbishop of Gulu to review, filed a copy inside a small cabinet on her desk.

Her goal, of course, was not to appease her superiors but to reach out to even more young women in need, women who had teetered on the brink of destruction, whose identities had all but slipped away under the control of the terrorists, and help them achieve self-reliance so they could take care of themselves and their children. Above all, she aimed to restore their dignity.

But Sister Rosemary had a long road ahead of her. She hadn't yet seen the worst.

CHAPTER EIGHT

MY SISTER'S KEEPER

LRA soldiers

Sister Rosemary was cooking alongside one of the girls in the kitchen when the young woman asked for a moment of her time.

"All right, let's go someplace where we can talk," Sister Rose said, leading the girl to the nuns' house and closing the door.

"Sister, the girl who shares my room—I don't think I should stay with her," Valerie said. "Can you move me somewhere else?"

"Why?" Sister Rosemary asked, half expecting to hear about a petty conflict between roommates.

"Because," the young woman mumbled, "I just realized who she is. I helped the rebels kill her parents."

Valerie was living in a rehabilitation center in Lira, about fifty-five miles south of Gulu, when Rosemary got a call from one of the women running the place. "Sister Rosemary, there are two young people here from the Sudan and they don't speak the language, so we don't know how to find their relatives. Do you speak Madi?"

The nun immediately thought of the unwanted orphans in Moyo, who knew no one but each other and were terrified of strange people in a strange place. "Yes, I'll come talk to them."

At the center, Rosemary found a young boy and a teenage mother with a baby barely one month old. LRA rebels had abducted Valerie from northern Uganda a few years before and taken her to Sudan. She had finally escaped just one week after giving birth, a gun in her hand and little Joy on her back, and been rescued by government soldiers with other escapees wandering the bush. The boy had been kidnapped from an orphanage run by the Sisters of the Sacred Heart in Adjumani.

Stunned that someone could speak her dialect, Valerie bonded with Sister Rosemary almost immediately. "Would you like to come with me to St. Monica's?" Rosemary asked. "You can study there."

The girl nodded. "Yes, I would like to go with you."

"Let me take them to live with us," Sister Rosemary told the manager of the center. "And one day we can take them back home."

A week later, the release papers were approved and the children arrived at the school with little more than a crying baby and a few ragged articles of clothing.

Valerie's words chilled Sister Rosemary to the core. "You killed her parents? How?"

Trembling, the girl began to explain. Kidnapped at a young age, she had trekked with other captives through miles of grassy wilderness, the guns of their militant captors aimed at their backs, until they crossed the Ugandan border. Reaching a populated village in Sudan, they were commanded to attack the unsuspecting residents and steal valuables from their homes. She would not reveal the method they used but would only say they were forced to kill mothers and fathers, brothers and sisters "in the most brutal way."

Valerie hung her head in shame. "I participated in it, and this girl I am sharing a room with—her parents were in that village. Now she is helping me take care of my baby. I feel so bad, and the guilt of what I did is killing me. I can't sleep in the same room with her. What if she finds out?"

Sister Rosemary's heart ached and her mind raced with the thought of how this might end. It was hard to imagine what the young mother had endured and the inner struggle she must be grappling with now. Then suddenly, Sister Rosemary knew what she needed to say.

"Don't be afraid. Tell her what happened. She may be upset at first, but she will understand because she was forced to do the same to other people. So she knows what it's like, and she will forgive you.

"And please try not to blame yourself for what you did. The two of you are not so different. You are alike in many ways, and God loves you both. You have an opportunity to minister to each other. You are sisters now."

Word gradually spread among the girls that, although she strictly enforced the rules at St. Monica's and expected them to work hard at their studies, Sister Rosemary offered a safe repository for their secrets, no matter how dark. One by one, the "formerly abducted persons," as they were called by relief organizations, came to her with their stories of trauma and courage.

One of three children in her family kidnapped by the rebels, Sadie was nine years old when she was snatched from her boarding school and forced to become a *ting-ting*, a babysitter to the younger children and a mule for transporting heavy supplies. Forbidden to eat the sacks of food she was forced to carry and foraging for leaves in the bush to ward off starvation, she was expected to smile in the presence of the soldiers or else be accused of planning her escape. At night, she and the other abductees slept in a row on the hard ground, their waists tied together with a strong rope.

On her second day with the rebels, the soldiers sent Sadie to accompany a young male abductee whom they had ordered to kill a man they considered their enemy. Such commands were commonplace, part of the ritualistic brainwashing process designed to retain "recruits." If the recruit failed to carry out the order, he or she would be shot to death.

"Why are we killing this man?" the brave girl asked her companion when they were out of earshot. "One day they may send someone to kill *us*! We should let him go."

Whispering as they drew near to their victim, the two came up with a plan. "Run! Run for your life!" they urged the startled man. "We don't want to kill you. Run!" When he was gone, they discharged a single bullet into the trunk of a tree.

"Did he shoot the man?" the rebels asked, checking the gun chamber when the pair returned to the camp.

"Yes, he killed him," Sadie lied. To her relief, the LRA soldiers never learned the truth.

Julia shared even more details about life in the bush. Born in Alero, a small town on the outskirts of Gulu, she was the oldest of three girls, all seized by LRA soldiers one night as they slept in their beds. Julia was convinced they were going to die even though, at the time, she had no way of knowing that two of her female cousins had been captured and killed the same day.

For the next two years, Julia served the rebels, first as a cook and later as a workhorse charged with transporting loot from the villages. After marching a great distance to the Garamba National Park in northeastern Democratic Republic of Congo, where Congolese and Sudanese soldiers would later clash with

Joseph Kony's men, the teen girls were randomly distributed as wives to their captors. There, in one of the world's most beautiful expanses of grasslands and forests, near a riverbank inhabited by wild elephants, giraffes, hippopotamuses and critically endangered white rhinos, Julia was forced to have sex with her new "husband" or face death at his hands. She was sixteen when she gave birth for the first time.

The soldiers in Julia's camp obsessively listened to their portable radios in an effort to keep up with the whereabouts of the Ugandan Army. Fearing that government troops would attack their hiding place in the Garamba forest, the rebels created a diversion, splitting the caravan into several smaller ones and ordering the captives to walk in different directions to avoid detection. Julia walked many miles to Arua, on the border with northwestern Uganda, carrying her baby on her back until she became too weak to walk. Seeing that the young mother might soon collapse, an older woman abducted by the rebels many years earlier toted the child for a while to let Julia rest. *If I die*, Julia thought, *at least there will be someone to take care of my baby.* It was not uncommon to find one lactating mother nursing the infants of three or four other women who had succumbed to disease, died in childbirth, or suffered serious injury and been left behind, bleeding and near death.

To pass time, the rebels enjoyed playing cruel games with their captives.

"Do you have money?" they asked. "What about food?"

If the abductee responded by saying, "I don't have anything to give you," the soldiers asked, "Do you want us to give you a t-shirt?"

When the innocent boy or girl answered "yes," the rebels would cut off an arm. If the child asked for a long-sleeved shirt, the guerillas would chop off her hand at the wrist. Sometimes the captors posed another trick question: "Do you want to continue speaking?" When the teenager said "yes," they would padlock his lips or slice them off entirely.

Even in the face of such mutilations, the prisoners were not allowed to show weakness or fear. If they did, they risked being put to death. Julia remained calm, at least on the outside, and was never forced to kill even though she was trained to do so.

"If we remain here, we're going to die," she confided in one of the other girls. "It's better for us to try to escape and leave this place."

At first her friend was too scared to try, but eventually she relented and agreed to run away with Julia. One day, when the soldiers were distracted, the two girls bolted into the forest with their children, making their way from Arua across the Albert Nile River to the Ugandan Army barracks near Atiak some 137 kilometers, or eighty-five miles, away. Government soldiers took Julia to Gulu, to a rehabilitation center for war-affected children run by GUSCO (Gulu Support the Children Organization), a non-governmental group helping reintegrate the child soldiers into society. Counselors encouraged her to forget the past, to move on, but the trauma weighed too heavily on her mind and she thought of little else. A year later, she was sent home.

For two years, Julia attended school in her home village of Alero but, haunted by what she had seen and done in the bush, could barely concentrate on her studies. Desperate to rid herself of the painful memories and start over, she had almost given up hope for a new life when she heard the radio announcement inviting formerly abducted girls to Saint Monica Girls' Tailoring Centre.

Julia was one of the lucky ones. Most of the time, when the girls returned home from captivity, an occasion that, under other circumstances, would have been cause for joyful celebration, life was never the same. The FAPs were commonly treated as spiritually "unclean" because they had participated, albeit unwillingly, in rebel activity and born children to the men who had kidnapped them. The young women who had been raped or otherwise forced into sex with their "husbands"—most were assigned as wives to the soldiers of a certain "rank" as soon as they reached puberty—were blamed for provoking the violence and considered spoiled and unsuitable for real marriage.

Knowing they had been trained to fight and take part in the bloody massacres, the villagers feared and accused them of being infected with *cen*, an evil spirit that could cause them to turn violent at any moment. A young woman who had committed atrocities under the watchful eye of her commanders was now considered a bad omen for the whole village and was sometimes tortured along with her children.

"Don't come home," suspicious townspeople sometimes warned on the radio. "If you come home, you will be killed." The rebels, of course, used their own scare tactics to keep the captives from escaping and convince them that no one wanted them back. All too often, they were right.

Not surprisingly, it was difficult to remarry with any lasting success. Husbands who had never experienced life in the bush were often unable to relate to what their wives had been through and eventually abandoned them, while in-laws were known to ostracize the women and verbally, if not physically, abuse them. Even the girls' own parents viewed them with suspicion and frequently refused to welcome them back into the family home.

Over and over, Sister Rosemary listened as the girls shared their painful memories of the past. But perhaps the most gut-wrenching story came from Sharon, who was just thirteen years old when the rebels kidnapped her and forced her to do the unspeakable. Sister Rosemary tried hard to mask her own sadness as she listened to the girl recount what she had endured in the bush. It was hard not to cringe.

A native of what was then known as Amuru District, twenty-five miles southwest of Gulu, Sharon was sleeping in the same room with her younger siblings when the door slammed open, waking them all.

"Come on, let's go! Get up!" The deep voice did not sound familiar.

One of the little ones started to cry. "Daddy? Is that you?"

Rubbing her eyes, Sharon realized this was not her father. Neither was the second man who entered the room with a gun.

After rounding up the children and their parents, the rebel soldiers pushed the frightened family out the front door and into the dark street. Sunrise was still an hour away. Other villagers, mostly children under twelve, were milling about in confusion as more of Kony's men lined them up for the march to Atiak. It would be the last time Sharon saw her mother and father alive.

"Pick one of them up and carry them," the soldiers ordered the older children, pointing to the youngest. "If you are not able to carry them, you will have to kill them. We don't want them slowing us down." Sharon bent down to allow one of her little sisters to climb on her back.

All day and into the night, the LRA militants, who had already attacked the local military base and killed several troops before infiltrating the village, herded the terrified civilians into the bush. They commanded the children, whom they had bound together with rope, to haul their luggage, cooking utensils, and large sacks of salt, sugar, millet and beans.

After many miles, they came upon a muddy, waist-deep river. Exhausted and sore, Sharon set her younger sibling down on the bank to catch her breath. "Can you help me?" she asked one of the rebel leaders. "I don't think I can cross the river with my sister on my back."

The man nudged her with the toe of his boot. "If it is too hard for you to carry your sister, we will throw her in the river," he snarled. "On second thought, if you cannot cross the river with her, you must kill her yourself. You must cut her in pieces."

Sharon looked down at the face of her sister, wide-eyed and innocent, and shook her head in dismay. What would her life be like if she murdered her own flesh and blood? How could she go on?

"Then we will kill *you*," the soldier announced. "It is your choice."

Placing the knife in her small hands, the man showed her precisely where to stab her younger sibling: in the liver, the neck, the head. There was no time to think, nowhere to run. *I hope God can understand and forgive me*, Sharon thought. That simple prayer would creep into her thoughts for years to come.

When she had carried out the order, the group trudged into the river, leaving her sister's lifeless, bloodied body behind on the riverbank. Her other sister, brothers and stepsisters were nowhere to be found.

The long march to the Sudan via the town of Atiak in northern Uganda was a grueling one. Walking with no shoes, their feet miserably swollen, the children stumbled along, trying hard not to speak. If they complained or were unable to walk on their own or carry their burdens, they were immediately shot and left to die. When the rebels sensed that the government soldiers were waiting nearby, they ordered the little ones to lie down and crawl on their stomachs through the tall grass with the luggage and loot of their captors tied to their waists. Now and then, a wild animal would leap from the thickets, attacking one of the children.

Sharon soon learned there were three types of LRA soldiers: the "kind people," those who showed no extreme cruelty; a second group who committed minor crimes against their victims; and the real killers who appeared to harbor no conscience when it came to torturing or exterminating any and all who got in their way.

Each evening, when the tattered entourage stopped to set up a temporary encampment, the rebel commanders instructed the older children to boil water for coffee in a large jar and prepare a stew of *ugali*, a millet-based porridge made with beans or groundnuts. Great care was taken to ensure that the rising smoke remained out of sight, but the abductees were seldom allowed to eat what they cooked except for meager remains scraped from the commanders' plates. Occasionally they were given one cup of cooked beans or millet to last them all day.

"This is for someone bigger than you," the rebels growled when the hungry youngsters stared too long at the food. "Don't touch it. Go pick some fruit."

The soldiers didn't know, and didn't care, if the wild leaves or seeds were poisonous. "Eat these," they said, pointing to an unidentified shrub with red berries, "and you'll survive."

One night as the commanders' meal boiled in a heavy iron pot, the soldiers suddenly sprang to their feet. "Quick! Move everything!" they shouted to the young girls. "Someone is coming to attack us. We must move. Carry the pots on your heads and keep walking. Hurry! And no complaints!"

Confused, Sharon stared at the boiling *ugali*. "Go!" shouted one of the soldiers, poking the butt of his AK40 into her ribs. "Do you want to die?"

Obeying the order, the thirteen-year-old lifted the white-hot pot with her bare hands and placed it atop her head. Searing pain ripped past her ears and through her small body as tears streamed down her cheeks. The smell of singed hair, which nearly eclipsed that of the food, would eventually subside but the physical and emotional scars would never go away.

One week after leaving Atiak, Sharon's group reached the River Unyama. After crossing the waterway, the captives were taken to Sudan, where they entered the camp of Vincent Otti, Kony's deputy. Otti had risen in rank to lieutenant general soon after the LRA was formed and was now second in command, answering only to Kony.

Under Otti's direction, the abducted children were trained to be soldiers in the Lord's Resistance Army. They learned how to creep under cover of thick grass, crawling on their bellies so as not to draw attention, and to climb trees with such stealth that even the smallest branches remained completely still, undisturbed by their movements.

"You are surrounded by enemies so you must learn how to protect yourselves," the rebels said, poking assault rifles into the hands of the teenagers. The guns, however, were emptied of bullets until it was time to raid the next village, when new captives were taken and the child soldiers were expected to kill those who put up a fight or refused to comply. The "recruits" were divided into three groups—one to ambush the villagers, another to spy on their fellow soldiers, and a third to pillage from their victims.

Sharon often heard Otti talking to Kony by satellite phone, receiving direct orders for the next attack. A common tactic was to find a group of strangers walking in a village, stroll with them as if they were acquaintances, then suddenly shoot them all. It was easy for Sharon and the other girls to hide their guns under their baggy skirts.

"Kill anyone. It doesn't matter who," the leaders said. "If you find a person digging with a hoe, take the hoe and beat him with it. If you find someone using an ax or a machete, use it to chop off his head. Make sure you report to us how many people you kill. The more people you kill, the better. Just do it as quickly as possible, before anyone can identify you."

Sharon knew what she was doing was terribly wrong, but the LRA kept her and the other child soldiers in check through calculated intimidation. "You can never go home," they said. "You have killed many people and stolen much property, and you are now enemies of the people. No one else will want you, and the government soldiers will kill you if you go back. You belong with us now."

It was in Otti's camp that the lottery took place. One day, the rebels removed their t-shirts and tossed them into a pile. Assembling a dozen female abductees and commanding them to form an orderly line, the soldiers instructed each one to pick a shirt, then step aside. When the girls had done as they were told, each man stepped forward and stood next to the captive who held his t-shirt.

"Come," said Sharon's new "husband," one of the oldest in the group. It was the same man who had ordered her to kill her sister at the river's edge. "I'll show you the house where we are going to live."

The man had shown no more violence to her since their arrival at the camp, so Sharon naively thought he was going to take care of her and protect her like a father. That night, he savagely raped her in their hut. From then on, if she refused to have sex with him, he beat her into submission. At sixteen, she became pregnant with her first child and bore him a total of three babies during her time in the bush.

After a while, the soldiers ran out of food and gathered the abductees for the long march back to Uganda, where they were ordered to steal as much as they could carry.

"You must each kill at least five people here," the rebel leaders instructed when they stopped at a small village not far from Gulu. "You will come back and report to us how many you killed." Sharon managed to murder four villagers but the fifth one escaped by running past her and knocking her to the ground. She was relieved he got away, a fact she did not share with her captors.

Five years after the rebels kidnapped Sharon from her home in Amuru, she began plotting her escape with two other girls. A few times, when she and her friends were sent to fetch water from a stream, they stayed longer than usual, pondering ways to distract their captors or hide in the forest after dark. Eventually their delays aroused suspicion among the rebel soldiers, particularly Sharon's husband, who forbade his wife from going to the river ever again. He started keeping a close eye on her during the day and, believing she might still make a break for freedom, decided to teach her a lesson.

"I think I need to put a sign on you," he said, carefully melting a plastic jerry can over the fire and allowing the hot drops to fall on her bare forearm, from the wrist to the crook of her elbow. The skin shriveled in a grotesque pattern and Sharon thought she might faint from the pain, but she held still. She knew what would happen if she resisted. "You can look at this when you think about leaving. There's more to come if you try."

Despite the brutal warning, and the fact that one of the three girls had withdrawn from the escape plans after deciding it was useless to try, Sharon was determined to get away.

One day, as the LRA rebels sneaked into a village, they were ambushed by government soldiers. As the rebels dropped to the ground in a rain of gunfire, Sharon and her friend ran as fast as they could, stopping only to tie their long shirts together with a rag so as not to be separated. Their rebel training served them well as they hunkered down in the grass, moving silently as one unit until the swath of material joining them began to unravel. After that, they held tight to each other with clasped hands, knowing their odds of survival were higher if they stayed together.

For nearly a week, the girls trudged farther and farther away from their captors, occasionally coming face to face with civilians who fled in terror at the sight of the child soldiers with their dirty faces, unkept hair and shredded clothing. By now Sharon had little more than a piece of cloth with which to cover herself.

"Rebels! Murderers!" people shouted when the girls tried to approach them. "Go away!"

Starving and shunned by everyone they met, one evening the teens discovered a deep hole in a garden and crawled in it to hide. All night and all day, they sat in the trench with nothing to eat or drink. "It's mango season and there are orchards all around here," Sharon's friend finally whispered. "Let's go look for some wild mangos."

Scampering to the highest branches of a nearby tree, they plucked armfuls of the ripe, yellow fruit and let the sweet juice dribble down their chins. Not far away, a woman was digging in the earth. Descending from their perch, the friends flopped, face down, into the grass and crawled to a spot a few feet from the woman. Turning to work the row behind her, she caught sight of the girls and bolted in fear, dropping her hoe.

"Don't run!" Sharon shouted. "We were abducted and we have escaped. Please stay!"

The gardener returned, her hands shaking. *Women often show more courage than men in the face of danger,* Sharon thought to herself. *This is one of those times.*

Sharon and her companion never knew why the woman was so overcome with emotion. Drawing closer to the girls, she began to cry, softly at first, then with deep sobs wracking her body. When she finally dried her eyes, she began to ask questions. "How did you get here? Where did you come from? How were you abducted? How did you escape?"

"I'm going for help now," she told the girls after they had summarized their stories. "There's a man cutting trees over there and he will help us."

"No! He will hurt us." Sharon no longer trusted men, no matter who they claimed to be. But the woman insisted and, when she was gone, the teenagers hid in the bushes, afraid the man would cause them harm or turn them over to the Ugandan soldiers.

When the farmers returned, the girls remained out of sight, watching. But the strangers were patient and waited for several hours, sensing the abductees would come back. When they finally did, too hungry to hide in the shrubs any longer, their rescuers were still waiting.

The kindhearted man took one look at the girls and shivered. Choking back his own fear of what they might do to him, he asked the child soldiers to follow him to his home, where he would call the local authorities. They would know what to do.

"In case these people are taking us to a bad place," Sharon's friend whispered as they walked the dirt path to the man's house, "let us make a plan now to kill them if we need to. At the first sign of danger, we should kill them. Or maybe we should just kill them now."

"No," Sharon protested. "We have to explain to the police why we did what we did in the bush. This is the only way. We were abducted and forced to kill people. We never did it because we wanted to."

Sharon and her friend were transported to the nearby Army barracks, where soldiers fed them and gave them fresh dresses to wear. She was then taken to the GUSCO rehabilitation center in Gulu and waited almost a month for her parents to pick her up. They never came.

Having received word of Sharon's escape, her aunt finally arrived to take her home to Amuru. It was then that the young woman learned both her parents were dead, slain at the hands of the same rebel soldiers who had kidnapped her family and killed all her siblings. Carrying the soldiers' heavy luggage on their heads, Sharon's parents had grown too weary to keep moving and been executed.

At her aunt's house, Sharon found it extremely difficult to adjust to normal life and leave the bad memories behind. She often obsessed over the horrors she had endured, playing them over and over like a moving picture in her mind. Sometimes, rage toward her captors welled up so thick in her throat that she felt she might kill again just to feel some relief.

Once while visiting the town center in Gulu, she overheard some girls talking about a place that accepted formerly abducted women with nowhere to go. But Saint Monica Girls' Tailoring Centre would probably not take her in, she thought. She had seen and done far too much.

A few weeks later, while she was attending church in Anaka, about fifty-four kilometers from Gulu, the priest made an announcement: "Any and all girls who were abducted by the rebels are welcome to enroll at Saint Monica Girls' Tailoring Centre and learn a trade. Their children are welcome as well."

Staring at the admission form—since no one was ever turned away, not even those without a proper base education, the paper merely symbolized admission into the school—she had trouble believing there was a place for women who were traumatized from the war, who had been kidnapped before they could finish their schooling, who had done terrible things. Women like her.

Sharon arrived at St. Monica's with little money, few articles of clothing, and no school supplies. In class, she kept to herself and seemed to have difficulty expressing herself. The nuns couldn't help but notice that no one—no parents, no siblings, no other relatives—ever came to visit Sharon, and this caused her great pain.

In her tailoring lessons, however, the young woman who had never before used a sewing machine quickly rose to the top of her class and was soon making skirts, blouses, pajamas, shorts and shirts. She produced such quality work that she was assigned to the team stitching uniforms for other schools. To Sharon, sewing was a godsend because it helped her forget about the past, at least for a while.

But her spiritual torment never went away for very long. Her first prayer of the night, every night, was an act of contrition: *God, please forgive me for what I have done.*

Early on, Sister Asunta, the school's deputy administrator, had alerted Sister Rosemary to the girl's suffering, but Sister Rosemary was careful not to approach her too soon. Sharon kept her distance too; she had heard the director was "tough," and that word held dark connotations for someone who had escaped from the bush.

It took the young woman a year to muster the courage to speak with Sister Rosemary about her ordeal, but the story finally spilled out, along with a plea for forgiveness.

"You don't need me to forgive you," Rosemary replied, cradling Sharon in her arms and gently rocking her like a baby. "God has already done that."

Tears rolled down Sharon's face, washing away some of the hurt that had accumulated over the years. As she had many times in the past, Sister Rosemary allowed God to speak through her as she offered words of consolation.

"God loves you more than you think," she heard herself say. "He never remembers our past."

CHAPTER NINE

BRAVE HEART

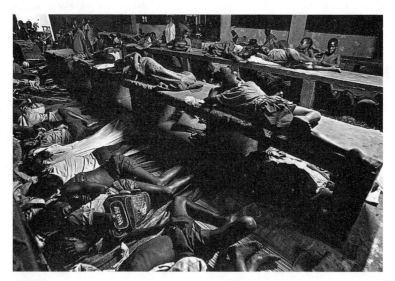

Night Commuters

B y 2003, throngs of displaced children were seeking refuge each night at Saint Monica Girls' Tailoring Centre, one of the first establishments to hide them from the Lord's Resistance Army. The Night Commuters, as they came to be known, walked miles from their homes each evening in search of safe places to sleep, far away from the scrutiny of LRA soldiers who scoured their villages after dark to "recruit" more young soldiers. Thousands of them—by some estimates, up to 30,000

Night Commuters scattered throughout northern Uganda—cowered in school buildings, churches and bus depots to avoid abduction.

Despite her anxiety about what might happen if they were caught, night after night Sister Rosemary hid the children under low beds and in oversized food containers. The rest of the nuns were even more frightened because, unlike Rosemary, they did not speak the local Acholi language and could not communicate with the strangers in their midst.

One day Sister Rosemary was doing some needlework in the living room of the nuns' house when a woman rushed in with two girls. One was fifteen, the other a few years younger.

"Sister, these are my daughters and I would like to leave them here with you."

Rosemary wrinkled her brow. "Why? You look healthy. Why can't you take care of them?"

The older girl began to cry, softly at first. Before long she was sobbing loudly, emotion shaking her small shoulders.

"What's wrong?" Sister Rosemary asked, turning to her. "Why are you crying?"

The girl continued to sob as the mother explained. "Sister, last night the rebels tried to abduct both of these children. This one," she said, motioning toward the weeping teenager, "was raped in front of me. And I couldn't do anything about it."

Sister Rosemary felt her heart breaking beneath the weight of the mother's words. It was all she could do not to break down herself. "Of course she can stay. Leave her here with us and we will take care of her."

The girl remained at St. Monica's, attending academic and vocational classes for more than a year before returning to live with her mother.

Had the rebels caught Sister Rosemary, they could have readily killed her and the other Sisters. A lone, unarmed security employee guarded the green gate at the entrance to the school and opened it for guests who appeared to be harmless, but it was nearly impossible for him to control every visit. When serious problems arose, even in the middle of the night, Sister Rosemary immediately called her sister Catherine, who represented President Museveni in Moyo as resident district commissioner. Catherine, in turn, phoned the commanding officer of the Ugandan Army in Gulu and asked him to drive out to the compound and troubleshoot.

Even when she found herself in the presence of one of the LRA soldiers, Sister Rosemary stood her ground, crossing her arms and protecting her personal space like a mama bear guarding her cubs. When rebels began to appear at the gate, attempting to strike up conversations with the young women who had lived in the bush, Rosemary instructed the gatekeeper, "Let me know if one of these men shows up."

One afternoon, Sister Rosemary discovered a few of her students kneeling at the feet of an LRA commander on the school grounds. It was the second time she had seen him here, greeting the girls as if they still "belonged" to his Army.

"Excuse me, sir," she said, approaching him with the same politeness as any other unwanted guest. "I'm asking you to kindly not come on this compound again."

The officer snickered.

"You make these girls feel like they are back in the bush, like they have to be loyal to you," Rosemary continued. "They are different now. They don't answer to you. Will you leave now? Can you do this for me?"

Like most of the Gulu townspeople, the soldier had heard of Sister Rosemary's tough-but-tender reputation. He studied her determined face, then shrugged. "Okay, Sister. Whatever you say."

Rosemary firmly planted her heels in the dirt and watched him stroll away before returning to her desk. He never came back to St. Monica's.

In 2005, the same year the International Criminal Court issued arrest warrants for five LRA leaders, including Kony and his deputy Vincent Otti, a number of rebel commanders returned to Uganda from Sudan in search of their "wives," whom they hoped to reclaim. Sister Rosemary was completing some paperwork in her office one day when a surprise visitor announced his arrival.

"Sister, I have come to collect my wife. Her name is Amelia." The young rebel officer, a hardcore militant by the looks of his uniform and demeanor, stood just inside the doorway, blocking the only possible exit.

"You have a wife here?" Sister Rosemary asked, silently praying for courage and the right words to say.

"Yes, and I want her back."

Rosemary already knew the answer to her next question. "Did you marry the girl you say is your wife?"

"No, but when we were in the bush, we were staying together. Now where is she?"

Sister Rosemary leaned forward in her chair. "Staying together is different from being married. Tell me, did you traditionally marry her? Did you pay the bride price, as is customary?"

"No, but her parents say I can stay with her now, in the village."

Sister Rosemary didn't budge. On the inside, she was shaking, aware that the girl could appear any moment and walk into a trap, or that another Sister could stumble upon the conversation and push the agitated soldier over the edge. Two nuns didn't stand a chance against a strong man with a gun bent on claiming his former sex slave. And with only one door leading to the outside—the one where the officer stood—there was no place for them to run. *Please God, don't let Amelia show up while we are talking*, she prayed. *Please protect her.*

"That is not marriage," Sister Rosemary repeated, standing her ground. "You used her when you were in the bush, against her will, and that is not marriage. So I'm asking you to get out and leave this place. You are not taking her with you. You have no wife here. You can go your way now."

The soldier scowled. For a moment, Sister Rosemary thought he might attack or ransack the building in search of his "wife." Instead, he muttered a few words under his breath and stormed out of her office, never to return.

Just as she had done years before in the kitchen at the Gulu convent, when the young rebel soldier startled her by removing the bullets he had tucked inside the oven, Sister Rosemary continued to show compassion even for her enemies. One evening she looked out the window and spotted two strangers by the gate, standing under the trees. They were dressed in government uniforms, but something about their appearance made her uneasy.

Exiting the house, she walked directly toward the men. She knew most of the legitimate Ugandan officers who sometimes passed by the school, but she had never seen these two before. "Can I help you? Is there something you're looking for?"

"We would love to find a place to sleep." The men looked like they hadn't bathed in days.

"Where are you from?" Sister Rosemary asked.

"Sudan." Their answer was enough to confirm her suspicion: They were rebels.

Vowing not to show fear, the courageous nun felt divine guidance working through her again. What she was about to do was bold, perhaps even foolish, but she knew in her heart it was the right thing to do. Perhaps they were plotting their own escape from the LRA, as many of the voluntary recruits eventually did.

"Follow me," she said, showing the men to a guesthouse where, in the basement directly beneath their room, young Night Commuters were hiding from soldiers just like themselves. Retrieving a set of clean sheets from the closet, she quietly prepared the beds and did not tell the other Sisters what she had done.

"Do me a favor," she said, closing the door behind her. "Please leave early tomorrow, before the children see you, because they will be frightened. They might think you're here to harm them, and I know you would never do that."

But at 8:00 the next morning, the door was still shut. The children who'd been hiding downstairs were already gone. "Sister, help us!" the men exclaimed when Rosemary knocked. "Sister, we are unable to open the door. It's stuck!"

Sister Rosemary reached for the handle and effortlessly pulled the door open. God, she knew, had been watching out for them all.

In spite of her positive attitude, Sister Rosemary was still human, and sometimes she felt discouraged, lonely and frustrated, almost to the point of giving up. Rehabilitating the girls at St. Monica's was an enormous responsibility, and she didn't always have the support she needed to carry out her mission. Sometimes, when parish priests who felt they should have more power began meddling in its operations, or when other nuns resented her authority, her efforts to transform the place into a healing environment seemed out of reach.

"Maybe I should abandon this work altogether," she confided in Father Luigi, who had remained her mentor and friend since their days together at the clinic in Moyo.

"Sister Rosemary, you have accomplished great things here," Luigi replied. "You can't stop now."

Father Carlos, a Comboni priest in the Gulu Diocese who had tried more than once to persuade the rebels to agree to peace talks with the Ugandan government, had known the benevolent nun since the outbreak of the LRA war in Gulu. "Sister Rosemary," he told her, "if you leave St. Monica's, we shall pack all the formerly abducted girls and their bags and follow you wherever you go."

Father Patrick, an Irish priest, and Brother Mike, who was from Germany, encouraged her as well. "You are doing what we should have done years ago but failed to do," Brother Mike said. "I am so happy to see that you are caring for these children, these young women. Please carry on and if you need anything, I will do what I can to help."

Sister Mary Magdalene, who worked in another mission, sometimes joined Sister Rosemary when she needed assistance with a project that required physical labor. And Sister Maryjina, a Sudanese nun who was now Rosemary's Superior, treated her more like a family member than a subordinate. Even so, it was difficult to remain encouraging in the face of such hardship.

"St. Monica's is very difficult to manage with so little money and no financial support from the Catholic Church," Maryjina told Sister Rosemary over the phone one day. "Why don't you close it?"

"No, Mother, give me a chance," Rosemary said despite her own doubts. "I'll do my best with what I have."

I will also do my best to get the word "frustration" out of my vocabulary, she told herself. *I just need to deal with it.*

Such internal pep talks were nothing new for Rosemary. Even as a little girl, her lighthearted attitude helped her shrug off her troubles and kept her from holding grudges. "Rosemary, it's hard for me to know when you're angry because you laugh so much," her mother Sabina had teased. "You keep on laughing when things are tough."

Even when she was scared or someone hurt her feelings, Sister Rosemary found a way to rise above it. At the height of the LRA war, however, something happened to shake her confidence to the core.

Since the beginning, when the insurgents began wreaking havoc in Gulu, her ability to be kind but firm, quick-thinking but level-headed, when she came face to face with the soldiers had protected her from danger, even death. But one day, when she was away on business in Kampala, she heard from one of the other Sisters that a certain rebel had threatened to kill her.

"I'm afraid to go back to Gulu," she admitted as she sat in the office of the Archbishop Nuncio, the Pope's representative in charge of the Vatican Embassy in Uganda. "I hear that someone is planning to take my life."

"Rosemary, go back. The church needs women like you," the Archbishop replied. "The school needs you. God will protect you. He always does."

All night, Sister Rosemary pondered his words and prayed for an answer. The next morning, she packed her bags and returned to St. Monica's. "If I die," she said out loud, "it means my work is finished. If I don't die, it means God has more for me to do."

1. *Starting a long journey of pain and hope-Gulu*
2. *Another orphan baby brought from Sudanese Refugees Camp-One day old*
3. *1978: In Midwifery School in Kalongo*
4. *Sister Rosemary in white t-shirt and Sister Jane in blue trousers digging with students at St. Monica's*

5. An abandoned baby with scar of a blade in the neck was brought to be cared for
6. Graduation in Development Studies and Ethics at Uganda Martyres University-Kampala
7. Graduation at Uganda Martyres University-Kampala
8. In England—Charles the young man who was encouraged by Sister Rosemary to abandon LRA
9. Sisters marching to a big church to make their vows

10. *Newly recruited girls learning to pray. Young Rosemary in middle row*
11. *Sister Rosemary poses with sisters who had just taken their final vows*
12. *Friends visiting Sister Rosemary and Mary Magdalen in Moyo*

13. *Sister Mary Magdalen, Dr. Santina Zanelli and Sister Rosemary in Moyo*
14. *1999: Sister Rosemary and Sister Alice*
15. *1993: In Verona*

16. *Young Rosemary*
17. *In Brussels—relaxing and reflecting on past experiences*
18. *1978: In Midwifery School in Kalongo*

19

20

19. *Sister Rosemary delegated by Superior General to accept the vows of Sister Marylyne*
20. *Rabbi David Zazlow, who nominated Sister Rosemary for CNN Heroes Award, looking through timetable of ceremony with her in New York*

21. *Orphaned children who felt Sister Rosemary was their mother*
22. *1993: Meeting a family she help move to England at the climax of LRA war*
23. *Daycare children who like to be lifted and loved*

25. Visiting a friend in Verona
26. Young Rosemary
27. Getting advice from her sister-in-law Diana
28. Housework is a way of relaxing

29. 1993: In England
30. 1987: Visiting friends in Italy who started supporting the Moyo Orphanage
31. The oven where bullets were hidden by a rebel
32. Bullets shot into a sack of flour

33

34

35

33. *Sister Rosemary showing the hallway where she and Sisters hid from LRA gunfire*
34. *Receiving a certificate of leadership as a guild speaker at the University*
35. *Idi Amin, President of Uganda from 1971-79*

36. *Sister Rosemary visiting Forest Whitaker at his school, Hope North*
37. *Artist's rendition of Sharon's little sister after being killed by her sister (from the documentary film*
   "Sewing Hope: The Story of Sister Rosemary Nyirumbe," narrated by Forest Whitaker)

38. 2008 CNN Hero Award

39

40

39. *President Clinton with Sister Rosemary at the Starkey Hearing Foundation Gala where Sister Rosemary was honored for her humanitarian work*

40. *All Pro NFL Wide Receiver, Larry Fitzgerald, Sister Rosemary, and President Clinton at Starkey Hearing Mission in Uganda*

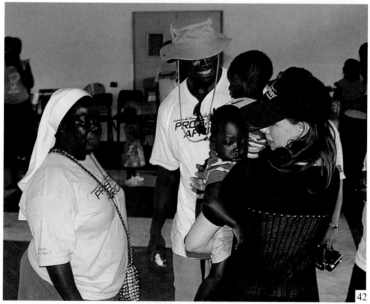

41. *NFL player Quinton Carter and Barbara Bush visit Sister Rosemary in Gulu*
42. *Barbara Bush and Quinton Carter visit the daycare in Gulu*

43. *Reggie Whitten, Sister Rosemary, Rachelle Whitten and Forest Whitaker*
44. *Actress Maria Bello proudly displaying her new pop tab purse*

45. *Actress Maria Bello, Sister Rosemary, President Bill Clinton, Forest Whitaker and Okello Sam*
46. *Actor and humanitarian Forest Whitaker, after introducing Sister Rosemary*

47. *Sister Rosemary at her school in Gulu, Uganda*
48. *NFL Pro Bowlers Roy Williams and Tommie Harris playing "Simon Says" with the young ladies at St. Monica's*

49

50

49. *Sister Rosemary talking to young orphans*
50. *Pros for Africa volunteers hand-digging water wells. Left to Right: Roy Williams, Ashley Harris, Mark Clayton and Nelson Peterson*

51. *Pop tab purses handmade at the school*
52. *Sister Rosemary teaching purse-making*
53. *One of the sewing machine rooms at St. Monica's Girls School*
54. *Pros for Africa Executive Director, Bill Horn*

55. *Sewing machines donated to Sister Rosemary's school*
56. *Purse-making at St. Monica's Girls School*
57. *Purse-making at St. Monica's Girls School*
58. *Young ladies sewing at Sister Rosemary's school in Gulu, Uganda*

59

60

59. Young ladies sewing at Sister Rosemary's school in Gulu, Uganda
60. Proud young ladies after being paid for purses they made

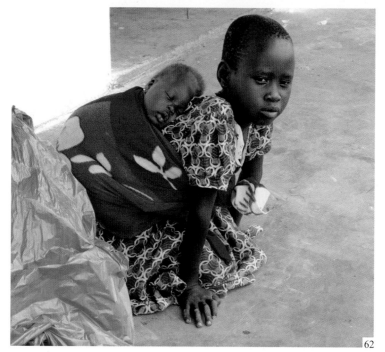

61. Sister Rosemary, Mark Clayton and Tommie Harris dancing with students at St. Monica's
62. Children caring for children

63. *The long lines at the free medical clinic at Sister Rosemary's school*
64. *Gerald McCoy, All Pro lineman for Tampa Bay Buccaneers, volunteering at Sister Rosemary's school*
65. *Adrian Peterson, All Pro Running Back with Minnesota Vikings, volunteering at Sister Rosemary's school*

66. *The long line for the free medical clinic put on by visiting medical professionals*
67. *Sister Rosemary and me speaking to a group of Oklahoma State Medical students*

68. 1995: Brandon and Reggie Whitten
69. All American Wide Receiver Mark Clayton, Sister Rosemary, Reggie Whitten and Nelson Peterson at ribbon cutting for the Brandon Whitten Hall in Atiak, Uganda

70. *Sister Rosemary with one of the children of an abducted girl*
71. *Sisters United launch party*
72. *Sisters United purses, all handmade by the young ladies at Sister Rosemary's school*
73. *A young mother working on a pop tab purse*

74. *Sister Rosemary, Reggie (PFA Founder) and medical students/ nursing student from both Oklahoma State University and University of Oklahoma*
75. *A child raising a child in Northern Uganda*

76. Okello Sam, Sister Rosemary and actor and humanitarian Forest Whitaker
77. Students from the University of Oklahoma and Oklahoma State University who were volunteering
   in Gulu, Uganda

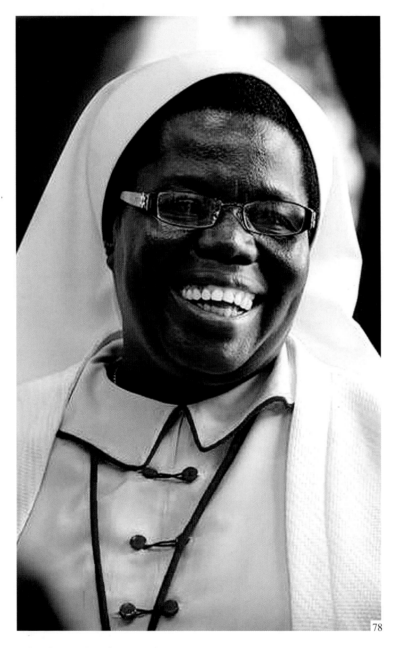

78. Sister Rosemary Nyirumbe

79. Sewing Hope documentary filmmaker Derek Watson in Uganda
80. Reggie Whitten at the daycare

81. *Left to Right: Tani Austin, Bill Austin, Sister Rosemary, Chelsea Clinton and Larry Fitzgerald*
82. *Roy Williams reflecting on an experience in Uganda with Sister Rosemary and Reggie Whitten*

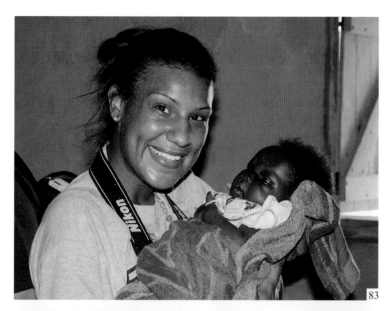

83. *Ashley Firmin Harris, namesake of the new school in Torit, South Sudan*
84. *Rachelle Whitten and Sister Rosemary during the early stages of Sisters United*
85. *Reggie Whitten, Dr. Suben Naidu, Mike Hinkle and John Hargrave in Uganda*
86. *Sister Rosemary*

87. Sister Rosemary prays at Brandon Whitten's gravesite in Oklahoma
88. Rachelle Whitten, Barbara Bush and Quinton Carter visit the daycare in Gulu

89

90

89. *Quinton Carter and Barbara Bush at St. Monica's*
90. *Pros for Africa NFL Athletes with Reggie's Stepson Jonathon in Africa*

91. *NBA players, Kevin Durant and Serge Ibaka attend a fundraiser in Oklahoma City for Pros for Africa with Sister Rosemary and Nancy Lieberman*

92. *Sister Rosemary with Rachelle Whitten, Serge Ibaka, Kevin Durant and Nancy Lieberman*

CHAPTER TEN

CHILDREN OF MURDERERS

Children playing at St. Monica Girls' School

As more and more formerly abducted girls enrolled at Saint Monica Girls' Tailoring Centre, the school grounds filled with children, many of them conceived with rebel soldiers in the bush. Like their teen mothers, few of the youngsters were readily accepted into society and many were considered harbingers of bad luck. They were the perfect scapegoats for the villagers' justifiable wrath against the Lord's Resistance Army.

"Rebel children!" the townspeople shouted when they spotted the outcasts at the town market or in the street. "They are the children of Joseph Kony, walking among us. We should kill them like chickens."

In a culture where regional clan members were apt to shun those who were different in any way, the young mothers feared for their children's safety and worried the people might take revenge on them. For some of the young women, the angst was so great that they felt it was better to abandon their children rather than subject them to the ire of a new family that refused to welcome them into the household.

A former abductee was faced with another dilemma. If she married a man after escaping the LRA, the new husband and his family would likely reject his stepchildren; if the woman stayed single, she faced severe economic challenges trying to raise her offspring by herself. A majority of the mothers chose not to marry in order to lessen the violence against their daughters and sons.

The FAPs who came to St. Monica's could hardly believe there was a place, and a group of people, willing to accept them *and* their babies without hesitation.

"Your children will be safe here," Sister Rosemary soothed, and she meant every word. "We will not allow the people to take their revenge out on them."

Sometimes, however, it was the young mothers who posed the greatest threat. Overwhelmed by their pent-up resentment and rage against the brutal men who had stolen their innocence, they sometimes hated their children for who they were—

constant reminders of a life they'd rather forget—and became verbally or physically abusive toward them. Now and then, one of the girls even attempted to kill her own child.

"We must help these girls learn to love the children they had with the rebel soldiers," Sister Rosemary told the other nuns at St. Monica's. "We must help them get past their anger. We must become more than just caretakers. We must become mothers to these girls. Let us be kind to them in order for them to be kind to others. That is what God wants us to do."

Regina, a young woman who hailed from Aywee, a small rural village on the outskirts of Gulu, had been abducted at age nine and forced to marry one of the LRA soldiers a year later. She had given birth to three of her four children while in captivity and escaped in 2003. Sister Rosemary found her in an Internally Displaced Persons camp and brought her to St. Monica's to study.

Sister Rosemary could tell that the girl was plagued with severe emotional problems, and she began to hear rumors of her violent temper. One day Regina's oldest child confided, "Sister, I am afraid. When our mother is angry she says she will set the house on fire and burn us all."

It took a long time, and much counseling, patience and love from the Sisters, but gradually Regina began to let go of her rage against her children, the world and herself.

Sometimes the children knew who their fathers were; sometimes they did not. Often the rebel soldiers used aliases and would not reveal their real names, nor where they were from, so the young "wives" never learned their true identities. Ellen, on the other hand, knew all too well who her "husband" was.

A beautiful girl with a round face and high cheekbones, Ellen was twelve years old when LRA militants kidnapped her as she walked home from school late one afternoon in 1994. "Drop your books," they commanded. "You won't need them."

The guerrilla gunmen ordered her to keep walking to her house in Atiak, where more rebels were already ransacking the family's possessions and rounding up neighborhood children for their army. Ellen screamed when she saw soldiers assaulting her mother, but she could do nothing to stop it. Her father was working in Jinja, the largest town in Uganda and the busiest commercial center next to Kampala, nearly 250 miles away.

Ellen's abduction from Atiak was both a blessing and a curse. The following spring, the Lord's Resistance Army would conduct one of its most brutal mass killings under the direction of second-in-command Vincent Otti, an Atiak native, in this small trading town near the Sudanese border. On the morning of April 20, 1995, after overtaking the Ugandan soldiers who were camped there, the rebels herded hundreds of men, women and children; forced them to carry their heavy loot; and marched them into a valley, where they stopped at a stream called the Kitang. Separating the captives according to gender, they proceeded to open fire on approximately 300 men and boys as the women, girls and elderly prisoners watched in horror. Otti then turned to the females and instructed them to applaud before ordering the LRA soldiers to select the next group of combatants and sex slaves from among the survivors. The Atiak Massacre, as it came to be known, was one of the largest mass executions in the twenty-one-year history of the LRA war.

For five long days, Ellen and the other young captives trudged through the tall grass, edging their way along hillsides that shielded them from view and slowed their pace, before reaching their destination in southeastern Sudan. Those who complained or stopped to rest were shot. "If you speak to any of your family members," the rebels told her, referring to her young aunt, uncle and cousin, who had also been kidnapped in Atiak, "you will suffer the same fate." Despite her overwhelming fear, her painfully swollen legs and the blisters on her feet, Ellen kept her hopeless thoughts to herself: *If I make it through this day alive, I will surely die tomorrow.*

Upon their arrival in Torit, Ellen was presented to LRA Commander Joseph Kony as one of his many wives—up to sixty young women, by some accounts, with whom he fathered numerous children. An average-sized man with black eyes and dreadlocked hair, Kony was unpredictable, laughing one minute, angry the next. He often moved as if possessed by a strange kind of spirit and seemed always to know what was going to happen next. Nevertheless, he was not particularly violent toward Ellen. Although she was desperate to escape the much older "husband" she had not chosen and return to her hometown, it was sometimes hard to believe this was the same man who would, by the time the war was officially over, be responsible for more than 30,000 killings, the abduction of as many as 100,000 child soldiers, and the displacement of two million people in his own country.

A few weeks after Ellen became Kony's wife, he looked at her and announced, "I think you are soon going to be expecting a baby." The prediction came true, of course. Ellen lived in Kony's house for eleven years and bore him three children.

She also trained as a soldier in a brigade of about 1,000. "You must learn how to use this to protect yourself," the rebel leaders said, handing her a gun. "You are surrounded by enemies."

The LRA's "enemies" were numerous: soldiers from the Ugandan government, other Museveni protestors who were not marching with the LRA, and anyone else who happened to get in their way. The training process was grueling, and some of the child soldiers died during a cholera outbreak.

Kony often called his officers to his elite assembly ground to give them their orders; those in the lower ranks never knew what was being discussed. He was a master at hiding his motives, his methods and his troops.

When Ugandan soldiers attacked the rebel camp in 2005, dispersing the terrorists and their captives, Ellen fled to Gulu with her daughters Bonnie and Mary. Her youngest disappeared in the chaos, but she managed to snatch up another woman's child after she was killed in the crossfire, and a week later they were back in Uganda.

Living in Atiak was out of the question. Years before, when her father returned from his work to find his daughter kidnapped and his home torn apart by the rebels, he had blamed his wife and accused her of being careless. At one point his grief nearly drove him to suicide. After a while, Ellen's mother decided it was best if she moved away and left him alone.

Ellen arrived in Atiak, eager to see her parents, only to find them separated. But that was the least of her troubles. When she was in the room, Ellen's father was affectionate with his grandchildren, but when she was out of sight he showed another, darker side.

"Never forget you are children of the bush," he muttered when he was alone with the girls. "You do not belong here."

In the village, people scowled and pointed fingers when Ellen's daughters walked past. "Children of murderers!" they shouted at Bonnie and Mary. "Look at the murderers!"

"Never tell anyone your father is Joseph Kony," Ellen warned the girls later. "It reminds them of things they don't want to think about."

Bonnie, the oldest, nodded. She knew that her father had done some very bad things.

In an effort to start a new life, Ellen moved with her children to Gulu and rented a house from a pleasant-natured woman of the Alur tribe. When they were settled, Ellen's brother and sister-in-law came for a long visit.

"Daddy! Daddy!" the younger children cried when they saw their uncle.

"He is not your daddy!" the sister-in-law corrected. "Don't ever call my husband Daddy. Your father is a murderer and he is still in the bush. You must live knowing that for the rest of your lives."

One year after Ellen escaped from Kony's clutches, she heard a radio announcement listing his former wives and requiring them to report to the office of the district commissioner. She froze when she heard her own name.

She vowed to ignore the instructions, and friends urged her not to go. Then one day she heard a knock at the door. Government soldiers had come to collect Ellen for a one-time visit with her former "husband," who had demanded to see for himself that all of his wives and children were unharmed before signing a final peace agreement with Ugandan officials. Ellen had no choice, but she took with her only the little ones who were too young to be away from their mother.

"I am satisfied that they are alive and cared for," Kony said at the meeting as the former concubines and their offspring were paraded in front of him and used as leverage by Ugandan officials. "I am ready for peace now. The time of fighting is over." Kony, however, failed to keep his word and never signed the peace agreement. Two years later, the diplomatic talks fell apart; by then the LRA had all but abandoned northern Uganda to carry out their attacks in the Republic of Congo, Sudan and Central African Republic.

In 2006, the same year she saw Joseph Kony for the last time, Ellen and her children went to Saint Monica Girls' Tailoring Centre, hungry and hoping for something to eat. She had heard about the nuns, and one in particular, who were willing to help women who had essentially grown up in the bush and who needed help raising their kids. She was surprised to find other former wives of Kony already living there, dismayed that most of the nuns didn't understand her Acholi language and, most of all, frightened of all the strangers milling about.

But she was determined her children would not starve. Initially, Ellen and her little family spent their days at St. Monica's and returned to their small house each night to sleep. The school was packed with girls recovering from their own personal nightmares, there were no available beds, and funds were extremely tight. Then one day, a nun introduced her to Sister Rosemary.

Now was her chance. "Can I please go to school here?" Ellen asked. "I can dig in the garden every day after class. I promise I will earn my keep. I want to learn, and I'm a hard worker."

Rosemary did not have the heart to turn the girl down. "Of course. Let's get you signed up for classes."

A few weeks later, a local man approached Sister Rosemary. "Who is this girl who keeps digging in the garden every day? Why is she working so hard?"

When Rosemary explained, the man quickly replied, "I want to help." For the next six months, he voluntarily paid for Ellen's tuition, food and rent, expenses that were generally subsidized by the school when funding was available.

Ellen kept her promise and worked hard at St. Monica's, both in the classroom and in the garden.

"Sister Rosemary, you know people don't like our children," she told the nun who had given her a chance. "I am afraid to leave them with babysitters because someone might take revenge on them, especially since Joseph Kony is their father. It is good that you started a school where we can come with our children rather than leave them with someone else."

Then she opened her arms and gave Sister Rosemary a big hug. "Thank you for helping us when no one else would."

CHAPTER ELEVEN

LADIES IN TRAINING

Daycare

Sister Rosemary noticed that when a young mother arrived at St. Monica's with her baby, she often brought with her a little girl to serve as a babysitter. Each morning the caregivers, most of whom were no more than four or five years old, clustered under the trees on the school grounds, cuddling fussy infants in their arms.

In Uganda, females were customarily raised to take care of other children from a very early age. But the thought of the little girls losing their own chances for education tugged at Sister Rosemary's heart. *This isn't right*, she thought. *These girls are wasting valuable time babysitting when they should be studying. They are falling behind in their education just like the abducted girls did when they were in the bush. And what will happen when the rainy season comes? They can't stay outside, and there is no place for them in our buildings. Where will they go?*

As usual, Sister Rosemary set about fixing the problem. With the aid of a Spanish priest who helped her acquire 5,000 Euros, she authorized the construction of a tiny daycare center, hired four mothers to run it, and enrolled the child babysitters in kindergarten. Before long, the building was filled with noisy babies and the classrooms were overflowing. *Lord, what have I done?* Rosemary prayed, chuckling at the same time. *What do I do with all these children?*

By now, Sister Rosemary's humanitarian work had won her a horde of allies across the globe. One of them talked to representatives from the Netherlands Embassy, who sent their ambassador to visit St. Monica's. "You have a lot going on in your compound. But what are your priorities for next year?" the woman asked when they met.

"Come, I'll show you." When Sister Rosemary opened the door to the cramped daycare center, several infants were screaming in distress. The staff barely had room to move. "This is my priority. I want a house where these babies can be cared for, and classrooms where the babysitters who came with them can learn."

Moved by what she had seen, the Dutch ambassador returned to her country and, bypassing the standard written process, approved Sister Rosemary's verbal request for funds for an expanded nursery and daycare. At 8:00 each morning, the formerly abducted women dropped off their children—infants at the nursery, older kids at the daycare and kindergarten—and picked them up when they finished their own classes at 5:00 in the evening.

Word of the beautiful new daycare center quickly spread, and other Gulu residents asked if they could bring their children too. More young mothers—not all of them had been abducted by the LRA—enrolled with their kids at St. Monica's. Spotting an opportunity to subsidize the cost of the service for her own students, who had no money to pay, Sister Rosemary agreed to open the center to the public and charge a small monthly fee. She had another motive too. Here was a way to start integrating the children from the village with those from the bush.

Despite the allure of a clean, safe place to house their little ones during the workday, many of the Acholi people harbored serious misgivings about letting their children mingle with those fathered by the rebels. "We would like to bring our children to study at St. Monica's," they told Sister Rosemary. "But we are afraid because you take in the children of Joseph Kony."

Sister Rosemary's response was gentle but firm. "The choice is yours. Either you bring them and you mix them with everyone, or you leave them all by themselves at home. It is you who will lose, not us. We will always be here for the poor, the needy and the orphans. That is our first priority.

"By the way," she continued, "we don't have 'children of rebels' here. We have children, period. They are pure and innocent and do not deserve to pay for the sins of their fathers."

A few skeptical villagers enrolled their youngsters in the kindergarten but were unable to get past their hatred of anyone associated with the LRA and silently withdrew them from classes. Then something miraculous began to take place, as the skeptics witnessed the children—those who had been sired by the rebels, and those who had not— peacefully thriving together in a safe learning environment. Peeking into the classrooms, it was impossible to tell the students raised in captivity from those who grew up in the village. Cheerful and innocent, the little ones got along well, without the bitterness hindering their parents. They were, as Rosemary had claimed, simply children. Perhaps the "children of murderers" posed no threat after all, the adults conceded as they gradually brought their sons and daughters back to the daycare center.

One day Sister Rosemary looked up from her desk and focused her eyes on the prison next door. She remembered what Sister Jane, a trained counselor at the school, had told her about the difficult conditions there, especially for the women and children, who lived in a section separate from the men. Their crimes ranged from petty theft to murder.

Hmmm, Sister Rosemary said to herself. *We are doing a lot to support disadvantaged women and children here at St. Monica's,*

and across the wall there are more women and children who have
challenges of their own. Maybe there is something we can do.

She quickly arranged a meeting with the warden. "Will you
let the women bring their children to our daycare center?" she
asked. "It will be free of charge. The children can stay with us
every day, as long as the mother is incarcerated."

The warden was encouraging, but this was not his decision
to make. "That is all right with me, but you will have to put your
request in writing and send it to the authorities in Kampala. I
am not allowed to do that."

Right away, the persistent nun wrote a letter to the
Ugandan prison commissioner, outlining her plan. Finding
Sister Rosemary's proposal hard to turn down—it would, after
all, save the government a substantial amount of money—the
commissioner agreed. Each morning, a guard accompanied
the female prisoners as they dropped their children off at St.
Monica's. Each evening, when they returned to pick up their
little ones, the children were clean, well-fed and happy from
playing all day. In their bright yellow uniforms, the women
reminded Rosemary of a long ray of sunshine pouring into and
out of the compound.

Later, with permission from the warden, Sister Rosemary
met with the women inside the prison. They giggled and
clapped their hands when they heard what she had to say. "We
are ready to give you more support," she told them. "What
kinds of things do you need?"

"Sister, we are so glad you are here," they replied. "One
of the things we need most is a change of underwear. We are

given one pair of panties when we get here, and we have to wash them each night. If they are not dry in the morning, we have to put them back on wet, and sometimes we get fungal infections."

As the women talked, the list grew: Wash basins, slippers, combs for their hair.

On Easter Sunday, Sister Rosemary and several other nuns from St. Monica's arrived at the prison with every item on the prisoners' wish list. "This is our gift to you," she said as the women danced with excitement, tears of joy streaming down their faces.

The Easter surprise wasn't the only gift Sister Rosemary had in mind.

"Do any of you know tailoring—dressmaking and cutting?" she asked on a subsequent visit.

Three women raised their hands.

"Where did you learn?" Two of the women had acquired their skills in town. The third had learned to sew at St. Monica's.

"You will be one of my teachers here, okay?" Sister Rosemary said to the young woman who had trained at the school. She never asked what crime the woman had committed. She didn't need to know.

Within a few months, the female prisoners were learning a new trade that could sustain them and their families for the rest of their lives. Sister Rosemary even taught some of the men.

In spite of her big-hearted efforts at the prison and elsewhere in the community, Rosemary continued to put her own students first. To the existing one- to three-year certified tailoring and catering programs at St. Monica's, she added agriculture and business administration. Brother Mike, a Comboni missionary who had shown his support from the start, secured a donation for five brand-new computers and a printer for the secretarial class. Throughout Uganda, St. Monica Girls' Tailoring Centre gained respect for its educational focus and came to be known as the only school in the country where administrators lived round-the-clock with students on the same compound. The formerly abducted girls continued to receive counseling and moral support, and were allowed to take as much time as they needed to complete their studies and remain past the unofficial three-year time limit if necessary.

Sister Rosemary and her staff worked hard to secure jobs for the girls when they left St. Monica's and, when possible, helped them acquire loans to launch their own businesses, often in tailoring or catering. After a while, the training center became recognized for producing quality workers, with local business owners and managers calling the school to inquire about hiring its alumni. Before long, nearly every hotel in the region had employed at least one St. Monica's graduate to run the front desk, cater special events, or cook in the kitchen. Other girls made a name for themselves with their tailoring; in the village market, they were often seen sitting cross-legged, sewing clothes for their customers. A few were hired as teachers at St. Monica's.

At graduation time, the students traded their school uniforms—forest green sweaters and skirts over white button-down blouses—for formal commencement gowns. Many times, the young mothers and their children received their certificates in a special ceremony on the same day. Once, Sister Rosemary wrangled sewing machines from her non-profit allies to send home with the girls. Another time, UNICEF commissioned the students at St. Monica's to produce small backpacks for schools in northern Uganda. When that project ended, the girls were allowed to keep the sewing machines as their own.

Slowly, even the most severely traumatized students began to make progress. A few became role models for the rest.

Jewel, the first formerly abducted girl to reveal her past to Sister Rosemary, the one who became the star seamstress in the pilot tailoring class, went on to start her own dressmaking business. Lily, who had been cynical about what she could accomplish at St. Monica's when she first arrived, completed her studies in two years instead of three, and later started a school for women in another part of Uganda. Sharon, the timid girl who had been forced to kill her own sister at the river's edge, began to open up and smile more. Sister Rosemary and the other nuns often called her to help them with tasks in their house, a special privilege saved only for the most trusted students. One day Sharon announced that, upon graduation, she wanted to stay at St. Monica's and work as a tailoring teacher.

Ellen, the beautiful girl who had lived in the bush as the wife of Joseph Kony, was a role model of a different sort. Hardworking and obedient, she completed the tailoring program at St. Monica's and went on to advocate for formerly abducted women, serving as chairperson of a group formed to fight for the rights of the girls who had been abused by the rebels.

Laura, who grew up in an Internally Displaced Persons Camp, was five years old when she was abducted along with her father, a former government soldier known by the LRA. "It won't be easy to travel with this child," she heard one rebel say to another. "Maybe we should just kill her."

When Laura's father heard these words, he struggled to break free. But his hands were tied tightly behind his back, so for now he would have to tame his impulse to run and wait for a chance to escape with his daughter. That chance came one day when the rebels untied his hands. Stealthily weaving his way to the back of the line, he eventually reached the end, where he scooped up his little girl and ran as fast as he could, carrying her in his arms. Only later did the LRA soldiers notice they were gone.

When she was older and her father could no longer pay for her education, Laura heard about Saint Monica Girls' Tailoring Centre and a group of Sisters who were welcoming girls forced to drop out of school for various reasons. There, as she learned how to sew and cook, Laura felt called to follow in Sister Rosemary's footsteps and become a nun. Selfless but ambitious in her quest for knowledge, she became a leader among her classmates, guiding them in their prayers while preparing to join the Sisters of the Sacred Heart of Jesus.

Not everyone, however, did well at St. Monica's.

Nina was running from her LRA captors when, during a government raid, a bullet from the crossfire shattered her chin, disfiguring her face. Unlike most of her classmates at the tailoring center, Nina lagged behind and never learned how to sew. Nevertheless, Sister Rosemary refused to give up on the girl and assigned her a small job cleaning the clinic.

Despite her compassionate nature and an infectious laugh that spilled from her lips at the slightest provocation, Sister Rosemary was a stickler for doing things right. To her, cleanliness was next to Godliness, which meant that the newly-washed floors must sparkle and the beds must be crisply made. In the classroom, she expected the girls to pay attention to detail and produce perfectly tailored garments. She had little tolerance for laziness or gossip and would not put up with lying or stealing under any circumstances.

Like a stern mother, Rosemary wanted the best for her "children," and she never minced words if a student took up with a man who didn't live up to her high standards. "What's your hurry?" she'd ask the girl. "Of all the men you have met, is he really the best? Why do you throw yourself at good-for-nothing men? You deserve more."

But when a girl's heart was broken, or she became pregnant by a boyfriend who abandoned her, Sister Rosemary was there with open arms, waiting to console.

Harriet, the daughter of Rosemary's sister Catherine, had always admired her aunt. Living in Martha's house as a child, Rosemary was more like a playmate than an authority figure to her nieces, at least in the beginning. Later on, she assumed the role of babysitter, friend and confidante; listened to their hopes and frustrations; and kept their secrets close. And as the years passed and her reputation grew as a caring, prolific nun who had managed to quietly gain respect for her work in a country with few strong female leaders, Sister Rosemary also served as a role model for her many nieces.

Harriet trained as a journalist and was hired as a radio presenter with the Uganda Broadcasting Corporation in Kampala, where she hosted a children's program, musical segments and cultural shows. After visiting St. Monica's in Gulu and watching Auntie Rose interact with the former abductees and their children, Harriet ventured the question she'd always wanted to ask: "Sister Rosemary, if you love children this much, why did you become a nun?"

"Well, that is my calling," Rosemary said matter-of-factly.

"But you have a mother's heart," Harriet protested. "How could you give up the chance to have your own children? Don't you miss having them?"

"No, Harriett, I am blessed with many nephews and nieces, like you. And I love being able to take care of the children who have no parents, who have no one to love them, who need someone to give them extra hugs and attention so they can be happy and healthy. Not having my own children gives me a bigger heart so I can have more children in my life."

Harriet paused. "But being a nun must be difficult."

"Not for me," Sister Rosemary said," because this is who I am."

In just a few years, the school population had grown from thirty students to nearly 250, plus about 250 children. It cost approximately 400 to 450 American dollars to support one girl and her baby for a year, little more than a dollar a day and not much by Western standards, but a lot of money for a poor nun with few financial resources and no aid from the Catholic Church. Funding was scarce. If the school kept growing, where would the money come from?

Sometimes a non-governmental organization offered to pay the tuition for a handful of girls. For Sister Rosemary, "tuition" was a relative term. If a girl could not pay her way at the school, she was allowed to perform chores to make up for it. The tailoring students were also expected to knit sweaters and sew uniforms for area schools in order to help bring in cash. To Sister Rosemary, the payoff was watching the young women succeed. Even after graduation, a girl was welcome to bring her children back to the daycare center every day for three or four years, free of charge, while she worked to secure a solid future for her family.

For a while, a group of lay volunteer missionaries from Italy made small contributions designated for specific items, but with the money came the stipulation that an Italian priest must oversee all expenditures. That didn't sit very well with Sister Rosemary, who ran a very tight ship but did not want outsiders deciding how many bags of millet or how many sewing machines she should buy.

Now and then, representatives from global humanitarian organizations questioned the school's policy of housing only girls. "Sister," they said, "we support your cause but you are discriminating against boys, so perhaps we should take our funds elsewhere."

"Listen," she told them, her hands on her round hips, her short hair pulled back beneath a white scarf. "I am not going to train boys here. Men have done terrible things to these girls, and the girls are afraid of them. It is men who have caused all their difficulties. Putting them in a room with boys who remind them of the torture they went through, who might have actually taken part in that torture, would be psychologically harmful to them and interfere with their healing process. There is no way I am putting them together.

"And besides," she added, standing her ground, "Some of the young mothers have boys of their own, so we *are* caring for both boys and girls."

Sister Rosemary was serving as a member of the Justice and Peace Commission in the Gulu diocese when the director of the Scottish Catholic International Aid Fund (SCIAF), Scotland's primary aid agency, heard about St. Monica's and decided to visit the school.

"Sister, can you tell us what you do here?" asked Josephine, a native of Malawi in southeastern Africa. Sister Rosemary sat down and began to describe the child mothers, then suddenly stopped. "Come. It is better to show you."

Josephine followed Rosemary to the small room where Valerie, the girl who had participated in the killing of her roommate's parents, was tending to her baby.

"This is just one of our girls," Sister Rosemary said, introducing the young mother. "Come, let me tell you about her."

Sister Rosemary and Josephine left the room, and the SCIAF director retrieved a pen and note pad before motioning for Rosemary to begin. "You talk while I write."

As the nun recounted Valerie's story—how the girl was abducted, how she had been commanded to kill the Sudanese villagers or be killed herself, how she had escaped only one week after giving birth to a "rebel child"—tears began pooling in Josephine's eyes. Before long, she was bawling, her pen quivering as she scribbled the story.

"Sister, I don't know how you have been dealing with this situation all by yourself. How have you done this without any help?"

"I really don't know who to turn to," Sister Rosemary replied. "I simply trust that God will provide."

That year, the SCIAF gave Sister Rosemary 17,000 pounds to help the women and children at St. Monica's. More funding followed in the years after that.

Sister Rosemary was truly grateful, but it still wasn't enough to feed, house and educate all the young women and children who kept pouring into the school. It would take a lot more to sustain her dream of a thriving vocational and rehabilitation center for hundreds of girls whose own hopes and dreams had been severed by the brutal acts of the Lord's Resistance Army.

It was going to take a fire stoked in the heart of a man across the Atlantic, thousands of miles away.

PART THREE

CHAPTER TWELVE

AN OKIE IN UGANDA

Reggie Whitten holding an abandoned newborn at the school in Atiak in 2010

L ike many Americans, Reggie Whitten knew very little about Africa when two friends started nudging him to go there. The successful Oklahoma City attorney didn't *want* to know anything about a continent 8,000 miles away, and he had no interest in going. What was the point?

Whitten's life had derailed just a few months before. Of his five children and stepchildren, his son Brandon had been the easiest to raise, and the one who caused the least trouble. The boy wanted to study law too, and practice with his dad, an easygoing "country" lawyer. It never occurred to Whitten that his perfect son, the handsome college football star, might be addicted to drugs until one night Brandon, while driving his girlfriend home after dinner, lost control of the car. The vehicle flipped, plunging the couple into a creek, where they dangled upside down for what seemed like hours. Lying in a hospital bed, his body battered and broken, Brandon admitted to his stunned father, "I was drinking, and I took a Valium."

Brandon healed from his injuries, but his beloved girlfriend didn't. Her death was something from which he never recovered.

For the next two years, he struggled to break free from his addiction. His father admitted him to a rehabilitation center, and that worked for a while, but overwhelmed with guilt and pain over the deadly accident he had caused, Brandon eventually began using drugs again. Willpower wasn't enough.

On February 15, 2002, the day after Valentine's Day, Whitten drove up on the scene of his son's fatal accident.

The flashing red lights startled Whitten as he turned into his neighborhood. Cars were pulled haphazardly on the pavement and a fire truck blocked much of his view. Shattered bricks littered the roadway.

Whitten didn't recognize the mangled motorcycle, a heap of twisted metal in front of the fire truck, about 100 yards from his house. Brandon's red pickup truck was parked to the side. It looked undamaged, but Brandon was nowhere in sight.

Police officers intercepted Whitten as he dashed toward the bike. "That's my boy's truck. Where is he?"

It was then that Whitten spotted a young man lying in the grass, crying but apparently unharmed. Whitten had no idea who he was.

"Brandon Whitten is your son?" the officer asked.

"Yeah. Where is he? What's going on? Is the guy on the motorcycle okay?"

The policeman motioned toward the young man. "Mr. Whitten, this boy here was driving your son's truck. Brandon was on the motorcycle."

The brick mailbox had exploded when Brandon, speeding at sixty-five miles per hour, smashed into it. He died in the air ambulance helicopter on the way to the hospital, the back of his head crushed by the impact.

For a parent, the death of a child is the worst horror imaginable. For Whitten, it was the beginning of the end. He would have done anything to save his boy's life—stepped in front of a train, a bullet, anything, to avoid the unbearable loss. Despite the fact that he had other children to care for, and a thriving legal practice, he could find no reason to live.

He stopped eating and quickly dropped forty pounds. His sleep, what little there was of it, was plagued by the details of Brandon's addiction and death. "I feel like I'm on fire,"

Whitten told concerned friends. "It feels like somebody poured gasoline on my skin and set me on fire."

Eventually he threw himself into his work, examining cases as if his own life depended on it. But the fix was only temporary.

The worst part was coming home. Brandon had rented his own apartment but still frequently spent the night at Whitten's house. Many times, the six-foot-three-inch, 270-pound athlete would race down the hallway and "accidentally" bump into his much smaller dad. It was like getting smacked by a freight train, but it was fun. Now, every time Whitten walked down that hallway, he automatically stopped to make sure he didn't run into Brandon, forgetting, just for a moment, that the days of their silly horseplay were over. He'd give anything to feel the wind knocked out of him again like that, just one more time.

Whitten's depression lingered, but his buddies were determined not to let their friend wallow too long in his grief. Mike Hinkle, an Edmond, Oklahoma, lawyer whose kids had grown up with Brandon, had been a close friend and advisor for many years. He had never been to Africa either but was planning a trip with J. Robert Hunter, director of insurance for the Washington, D.C.-based Consumer Federation of America and a former Texas Insurance Commissioner and Federal Insurance Administrator. Whitten had met Hunter when he called on him to testify in a deposition in a lawsuit. Sitting back in his chair, Whitten listened intently when Hunter was asked the standard opening question, "What do you do?"

"I do three things," Hunter explained. "Number one, I work as an insurance consultant. Another third of my time I spend doing pro bono work, advising the less fortunate about insurance in my non-profit organization, Consumer Federation of America. And I spend the other third volunteering in Africa."

Wow, that's pretty interesting, Whitten thought at the time. In an effort to find out more, he and Hinkle took Hunter to dinner and asked him about his work in Africa. Deeply disturbed by the merciless tactics of President Idi Amin, in the late 1970s Hunter traveled to Uganda, hoping to somehow make a difference. On the way from the Entebbe airport to his hotel, he was shocked by the hopelessness he saw in the people's faces; later, he was astonished by the "popcorn" gunfire that lasted all night in the capital city. Friends at a hospital where he was helping took him to the epicenter of the killing, Luwero Triangle, where he saw bodies piled up in an IDP camp, in plain view, next to the drinking water the refugees were forced to use. After investigating the details and trying for days to figure out a way to help, he realized he was making no headway and, frustrated, finally booked a flight back to the United States.

"Don't be too discouraged," said the young lady with whom he struck up a conversation at the airport. "Maybe my dad can help."

Hunter was skeptical. "Who's your dad?"

"Andrew Young."

Stunned by his good fortune, Hunter arrived in the United States with the personal phone number of the fourteenth

Ambassador to the United Nations, the same high-profile civil rights activist who was with Martin Luther King Jr. when King was assassinated in Memphis in 1968. The next year, Young accompanied Hunter on his second trip to Africa, and Hunter went on to become heavily involved in peacemaking negotiations between various African countries and raised money to build much-needed hospitals, dental clinics and schools.

Hinkle and Hunter weren't giving up. "Come on, go with us," they coaxed. "It'll do you good. It'll get your mind off things. You need a change of scenery."

Finally, Whitten grew weary of trying to stave off his friends and agreed to the trip, which would take place in November 2002, nine months after Brandon's death. A longtime history buff, he educated himself about Uganda by asking Hunter more questions and surfing the Internet. Until then, he had never heard of the Lord's Resistance Army and the savage war Joseph Kony had waged against his own people. *What a silly name for an army*, Whitten thought when he read about the history of the LRA. *What's the Lord got to do with an army, especially one like this? And how could one man kidnap this many children, turn them into soldiers and sex slaves, and force them to commit such brutal crimes?*

Whitten could hardly fathom the idea of such a militant group. Why had no civilized nation stepped in to stop this?

Scenes from the 1977 movie, *Raid on Entebbe*, flashed through Whitten's mind as the plane landed at the same spot where pro-Palestinian supporters held hijacked Israeli passengers hostage in 1976. Amin had apparently looked the other way and treated the terrorists like guests in his country.

One of Amin's former personal pilots met Whitten's group and gave them a tour of the airport. It was still riddled with bullet holes from the raid, which, to a guy from Oklahoma, was like seeing firsthand evidence of the famous gunfight at the O.K. Corral—frightening and thrilling at the same time.

Whitten was surprised by Uganda's natural beauty, its fertile lushness, and even more taken aback by the smiles on the faces of the children he saw in Entebbe. He soon learned that the nation's capital, with its fancy hotels and neatly paved streets, did not represent most of the country. Likewise, the two other African nations on their itinerary were starkly different from anything he would see in Uganda. In Kenya, Whitten played the role of the typical tourist, his jaw dropping at the sight of the "Big Five" game animals: African elephant, black rhinoceros, cape buffalo, leopard and lion. It amazed and unnerved him to see a 500-pound feline lounging three feet away. He was nearly as startled by the modern look of South Africa's Capetown, with gleaming skyscrapers that reminded him of New York City.

The morning after Whitten and his friends arrived in Uganda, they climbed into a beat-up Toyota for a tour. The streets leading out of Entebbe were jammed with old cars swerving erratically, almost as if they were trying to crash into each other. Bicycles loaded with three or four riders, plus their belongings—firewood, jerry cans full of water, even mattresses—clogged the roadways, while streams of people marched on foot like ants alongside them. The whole thing reminded Whitten of an amusement park bumper car ride.

The urban traffic soon gave way to the roughest dirt road Whitten had ever seen. Most of the *boda-boda* motorbike taxis carried two or three people on back, and a child perched on the handlebars. No one wore a helmet on the bone-jarring ride.

With much time to kill, Hunter told him about a remarkable nun who was making a difference in war-torn Gulu. In spite of the very real danger, Sister Rosemary Nyirumbe was running a rehabilitation center and vocational school there for young girls who had escaped from the LRA after living in slavery, often for years. To Whitten, her willingness to stand up to the rebels in spite of her short stature, when no one else would, sounded almost mythical, like that of a legendary hero in a story passed down from generation to generation. She sounded too good to be true.

Gulu was a small town dotted with dilapidated, one-story structures. Young girls, no older than nine or ten years, carried babies on their backs, all of them orphaned by the war. The adults, unemployed and incapable of supporting themselves since the LRA conflict began terrorizing their town in the mid-1980s, propped their starving bodies against rundown houses and skinny tree trunks and stared at the car as it drove past. They shared the same hopeless look Whitten had only seen in pictures back home.

Whitten was disappointed to learn that Sister Rosemary was away from her school, traveling on business, so they would have to talk with her another time. For a brief moment, his own pain subsided as he witnessed the plight of the children of northern Uganda.

I've got to meet this woman, he thought, forgetting, for once, about his own heartache. *I'll be back.*

CHAPTER THIRTEEN

PROS FOR AFRICA

Left to Right, Mark Clayton, Roy Williams and Tommie Harris

Reggie Whitten and Adrian Peterson, two of the co-founders of Pros for Africa, with Sister Rosemary in Atiak, Uganda

The death of a child leaves a deep wound that never completely goes away, no matter how much time passes. But gradually, Whitten began to feel better, to reach out to others, to put his own loss into perspective. The trip to Uganda had opened his eyes to the suffering of other people and helped ease his own pain. He was finally starting to heal.

The work of Sister Rosemary tugged at his heart. *How can I just sit here in the comfort of my home, knowing those children have been through so much?* he thought. *I need to do something.*

In early 2003 Whitten and his wife Rachelle made plans to attend the National Prayer Breakfast in Washington, D.C. The annual event, held each February since 1953, provides a non-threatening forum for political, social and business leaders to build relationships with their colleagues across the globe. More than 3,000 guests from around the world, including Sister Rosemary, would be there.

After the breakfast, Whitten met her at the home of his friend Robert Hunter, where she was staying. She was much shorter than he imagined, and he was amazed by the perpetual smile on her full lips. Whitten expected someone much taller, more hardened, not this sweet little nun who giggled at the slightest friendly remark. But he soon realized that a steely determination lurked beneath that congenial personality.

During their conversation, Sister Rosemary described how she learned to box with her brothers when she was a little girl, what it was like to grow up in a country where women's rights were virtually nonexistent, and how, more than once, she had stood up to rebel soldiers who threatened her safety and that of her fellow Sisters and students. *I'd hate to get in a fist fight with this woman*, Whitten mused as she talked. *She'd whip my butt.*

He felt a bond with Sister Rosemary almost immediately, and he was disappointed when his hour with her was up. Other guests at the house were clamoring to speak to her too.

A few days later, he called her at Hunter's house. "I want to make a donation to your school," he said.

"Thank you, Reggie," she replied. "Anything you can send will help. We are barely able to keep our doors open right now."

Whitten and his wife began sending personal checks to support Sister Rosemary's work. Sharing his wealth with those less fortunate—something he'd never thought much about—was like balm for the soul, a sort of spiritual medicine that soothed the ache over losing his boy. By helping someone else, his life made more sense.

Whitten later visited the school and Sister Rosemary in Gulu. It was depressing to see so many young girls still wandering the streets—sad, starving urchins with no parents to care for them and no place to go. They all shared the same thousand-yard stare, like Vietnam veterans who'd survived the horrors of war but felt dead inside. These girls, too, had witnessed the unspeakable and been forced to do terrible things by Kony's militia.

Sister Rosemary greeted Whitten and Hunter at the school and ushered them into a small conference room. "Please bring them a cold drink," she instructed one of the girls. "They've had a long trip."

The young woman returned with a pitcher of tea and two glasses. "Thank you," Whitten said, smiling and attempting, as Americans tend to do, to make eye contact. But the girl cast her eyes to the floor, bowed her head low, as if in church, and shrank from his friendly gesture. Whitten had never seen a more subservient posture. It was as if she were trying to disappear.

"Yes, she was held captive by the LRA and escaped," Sister Rosemary confirmed later when Whitten asked about the girl. "It's going to take a long time for her to get over it, if she ever does."

The girl with the tea wasn't the only one too shy to talk. As Rosemary gave the men a tour of the facility, many of the students hung their heads or looked away. Some pretended to ignore the visitors and kept sewing, washing their clothes or hoeing the garden. Occasionally one of the girls tried to conjure a smile. It was difficult for them to feel comfortable around men, especially strangers. Men, bad men, had shattered their self-esteem and scarred them for life. That fear might never go away.

In the presence of Sister Rosemary, however, they blossomed. She could hardly walk through the compound without at least one of them running up to her with a question or hug. She was a jack of all trades—part headmistress, part farmer, part seamstress, part mechanic, part doctor, but most of all, a firm but loving mother. It was obvious that the girls adored her, and that she felt the same about them.

It seemed as if there was nothing Sister Rosemary was too afraid to tackle. Once, when Whitten flew her to Oklahoma for a visit, the two had breakfast with one of Whitten's friends, a dentist.

"Sister Rosemary, what do you do when one of the kids at your school has a bad tooth that needs to be pulled? Do you have a clinic?" the dentist asked.

Rosemary laughed. "No, we don't have a clinic for that."

"Well, what do you do?"

"I pull it, of course."

The dentist looked horrified. "How in the world do you do that, without anesthetic?"

"We have a tool," she said. "It's sort of like what you would call pliers."

Her breakfast companion was stunned. "Oh my God, do you really do that? That thing could get infected."

Sister Rosemary gave him a stern look, as if he were a child acting silly at an inappropriate moment. "What do you mean? I can't let them sit there in agony. It has to be pulled, so I pull it."

Whitten continued to send money to St. Monica's and, although other individuals and NGOs offered support off and on, he and Rachelle became the school's primary benefactors and kept in touch with Sister Rosemary through email, cell phone calls and an occasional visit. Even when the school was in dire need of funding for sewing machines or medicine or the electric bill payment, she never asked for a dime, never pressured him for more. After a while, Whitten began to feel that their contributions simply weren't enough and he worried the school might shut down if he were unable to help. What if he and his wife ran out of money? What would happen to the school when they got old and passed away?

In 2007, the Whittens agreed it was time to formalize their support, and together they created a non-profit organization focused, at first, on making a difference in the world while honoring Brandon's memory. The initial goal was simply to set up a scholarship in Brandon's name, but that quickly snowballed into other charitable projects, all of which related in some way to Brandon's life.

When Whitten called Sister Rosemary to share the good news, she dropped to her knees and burst into tears. The Whitten-Newman Foundation was making a significant donation to St. Monica's—more money than Sister Rosemary had ever seen in her life, enough to keep the place going for quite some time. Repeating the words of the Blessed Virgin, Sister Rosemary prayed aloud as she knelt in her office, "My soul magnifies the Lord, for He has done great things for me, and holy is His name."

By 2009, Whitten was antsy to do even more. Helping the girls at St. Monica's had changed his life, kept him from sinking farther into the dark hole of despair. It had also, according to Sister Rosemary, kept the school from going under when food and other necessities were scarce. What if the Whitten-Newman Foundation broadened its efforts, ventured into other parts of Africa to provide aid?

"Don't you think that's a little too ambitious, Reggie?" friends asked. "Aren't you getting in over your head?"

It certainly wouldn't be the first time. Whitten had a history of shouldering tough challenges. But how would he raise the money? In America, a non-profit organization needed big bucks to lure attention through advertising, celebrity endorsements and Internet branding. The new African initiative must have a recognizable face—and a theme. Whitten decided to call it "Pros for Africa" to represent volunteer professionals of all kinds. His goal was to encourage doctors, lawyers, engineers, dentists, nurses, teachers, and yes, athletes, to volunteer to help Sister Rosemary and her girls.

Oklahoma is known for its cows, its oil production, its football players and its musicians, and not necessarily in that order, Whitten concluded as he pondered the possibilities. *Do I know any famous musicians? No. How many movie stars do I know? None. Do I have access to any well-known football players? Maybe.*

Whitten remembered that Jay Mitchel, a young lawyer in the firm, had played basketball at the University of Oklahoma before attending law school and had roomed with several members of the OU Sooners football team who went on to earn National Football League fame. Among Mitchel's friends were Mark Clayton, an All American wide receiver at Oklahoma who was later recruited in the first round of the NFL draft and played for the Baltimore Ravens, and five-time NFL All Pro Roy Williams, who played safety for the Dallas Cowboys and Cincinnati Bengals.

Mitchel introduced Clayton and Williams to Whitten, who immediately sensed that these were no ordinary millionaire athletes. The trip to Africa, he told them honestly, would be rough—no five-star hotels, no luxurious beaches, no nightlife. Getting there would take more than twenty-four hours via an oceanic journey to Paris or London, followed by a daylong flight to Entebbe and a grueling four-hour drive to Gulu. They would have to avoid drinking the water, sleep under mosquito nets, and accept the fact that the phone service would probably be unreliable. Before the trip, they would need seven or eight vaccinations; afterward, it might take them a week to recover from the jet lag and lack of sleep. And they would have to pay their own way. "Oh," Whitten added, "you'll be physically working your butts off, digging and building things and handing out food to people who don't speak your language."

In the fall of 2009, Whitten met Bill Horn, a local sports marketing agent who worked with Adrian Peterson, an All American and later All Pro running back from Oklahoma, who now played for the Minnesota Vikings and went on to become the NFL Offensive Rookie of the Year; All American and All Pro Tommie Harris, a bull of a defensive end for the Chicago Bears and, later, the San Diego Chargers; and a number of other NFL players. Horn began recruiting athletes to help Sister Rosemary and her girls, but he and Harris needed no persuasion. They had both done humanitarian work in Africa but were so touched by Sister Rosemary's story that they quickly agreed to become co-founders of Pros for Africa. Peterson joined the PFA team as well, and Horn later became Executive Director.

Only one of the professional athletes—Tommie Harris— had ever been to Africa. After talking with Whitten, all four were ready to go and excited about meeting Sister Rosemary. Although many of their fans in the United States worshipped them as heroes on the gridiron, each of these young men understood that the game of football was just a game. The real hero, they knew, was Sister Rosemary, who had risked her life to save innocent women and children from Joseph Kony and his LRA thugs.

Yes, the players had achieved greatness in their young careers and garnered much recognition: All-American status, a Lombardi award, a close call for the cherished Heisman Trophy. In the world of football, these guys were about as big as it got. But more importantly, these four young men were solid citizens and role models, and they cared deeply about helping others less fortunate.

As hoped, the formation of Pros for Africa triggered a frenzy of media attention, at least in Oklahoma. It didn't translate into a lot of fundraising success, but it did draw a number of volunteers—doctors, nurses, lawyers, water well engineers, teachers, and students from medicine and law—who stepped up to offer their services, free of charge.

In March 2010, forty-eight Pros for Africa volunteers made their first trip to Uganda. Boarding three basic rental buses—not the luxury vehicles the athletes and business professionals were used to—they made the long, bumpy ride from Entebbe to Gulu. By now, Kony and his men were supposedly hiding in Sudan or Congo, but no one knew for sure. Few visitors had ventured into northern Uganda since the war, and virtually no one had gone to help the young women who had been brutally victimized for so long. No one except a spunky Catholic nun who would sacrifice anything—her time, her energy, even her life, if necessary—to heal their damaged hearts.

When the volunteers arrived, Sister Rosemary was waiting on the school grounds, arms flung wide to hug everyone who stepped off the buses. The girls were waiting there too, to welcome their guests in traditional Ugandan fashion. Singing and jumping in unison, they performed a high-energy dance while vibrating their tongues in their mouths in a loud, high-pitched trill. Other villagers joined in, dancing and drumming on wooden *djembes* covered in animal skins. Before long, the Gulu residents had surrounded the PFA workers, who were awed by the unexpected reception and the beautiful, smiling children who clustered around them, not because they were well-known athletes—the kids had no idea who their high-profile guests were—but because they were Americans bringing hope. Here, they were not football stars. They were ordinary men come to perform ordinary labor, using their strength and size not to make touchdowns but to give critical aid to strangers in need.

The next day, Sister Rosemary took the volunteers to Atiak, where one of the most notorious LRA massacres had taken place. Thanks to Sister Rosemary's friends in Oklahoma, a second St. Monica's school was nearing completion there, seventy kilometers from the main compound. By the time the entourage reached its destination, Sister Rosemary was in tears, not from the difficult drive, but from watching the caravan

SEWING HOPE

follow closely behind her in what she had come to know as "the gospel of presence." She could almost hear a voice encouraging her, *You are starting another difficult journey, but you are not alone.*

In an act of great kindness, Sister Rosemary named one of the new buildings at Atiak the Brandon Whitten Hall in recognition of Whitten's son. Tears flowed when the ribbons were cut and the groundbreaking began. Out of a terrible tragedy had emerged a beautiful partnership between the Whittens and Sister Rosemary—an irony, they realized, and a blessing for all.

Before long it was evident that another important partnership had begun to take root. During the trip to Gulu, Whitten watched as a talented documentary filmmaker from Oklahoma named Derek Watson recorded the details of their visit. Technologically savvy, with a keen eye for details, the young man showed a remarkable compassion for the people of Uganda.

"Sister Rosemary is the most amazing person I've ever met," Whitten remarked as he and Watson watched her in action.

Watson nodded. "I agree. I've never seen anyone like her."

Whitten paused, then offered an idea. "Hey Derek, why don't we interview and record the testimony of Sister Rosemary and some of her girls? It would make a great film!" Watson enthusiastically agreed.

For the next three years, the men would collaborate to produce a documentary about the amazing life and work of Sister Rosemary Nyirumbe.

Back in the heart of Gulu after their trek to Atiak, the athletes rolled up their sleeves outside the St. Monica campus and went straight to work. Trading their numbered jerseys for simple PFA t-shirts, they dug trenches, gobbed mortar between rough-hewn logs to build rudimentary houses, and washed clothes with the children. Scooping cups of beans, rice and flour from plastic buckets into the grateful villagers' tattered bags, they were touched by the sight of old ladies bending over to retrieve each precious piece that fell to the ground.

Under the direction of volunteers from Water4 from Oklahoma City, another non-profit partner of Pros for Africa led by Dick Greenly and Chris Cotner, the athletes drilled one well and broke ground for five more at various sites, including the St. Monica complex, Sister Rosemary's home village of Paidha, and a nearby boys' school called Restore Academy. Taking turns and using hand drills—there was only sporadic electricity to the buildings, and none to the new wells, and in this Third World country there was no access to a truck with a gasoline-powered auger—the men twisted the pipes into the ground. One "modern" well was a godsend, but six constituted a miracle in a land where residents filled jerry cans with water from parasite-riddled streams that frequently make them sick, or worse.

Competitive by nature, the football players couldn't resist challenging each other to a friendly contest to see who could drill the longest and fastest. Dividing themselves into teams, they lined up—two men facing each other, one on either side of the T-shaped drill brace—then grabbed the handles and twisted the screw into the ground as fast as they could before handing it off to the next "player." Not surprisingly, when Harris and Williams, the bulkiest of the four athletes, were on the same "team," they easily won.

On their visit to Restore Academy, the PFA volunteer athletes played soccer with the young men, most of whom had lost their parents in the war. An attorney named Bob Goff, himself an inspirational figure who led the first-ever prosecution against a Ugandan "witch doctor" who made human sacrifices, had founded the school in 2007. He and Sister Rosemary were partnering together in their own way to teach dispossessed children a better way of life.

At the Academy, the NFL players passed out dozens of "water straws" made by another Oklahoma non-profit foundation called "Water is Life." The purifying straws allowed users to drink clean water from the dirtiest of streams.

As the kids watched in disbelief, Whitten placed an oversized blue "straw" into a plastic jug of dirty water taken from a nearby stream, tossed in some extra dirt, grasped the straw in his hand and began sucking from it as if it were filled with Kool-Aid. Then one by one, the athletes stepped up and did the same thing. When the boys saw that the "magic" straws, which purified the polluted water using charcoal filters and iodine crystals, actually worked, their grimaces turned into grins and they held out their hands. Soon, dozens of children were sipping clean water, a rare commodity in a poverty-stricken country where it is not uncommon for 100,000 people to share one or two primitive wells.

The volunteers, of course, spent much of their time at St. Monica's, assisting with various projects, including the expansion of the crude clinic originally constructed by the Scottish Catholic International Aid Fund a few paces from the house where the child mothers lived. With dwindling funds and support staff, the clinic offered few real medical services and was only open for emergencies, and only for the students.

Four PFA doctors—Al Moorad, Suben Naidu, Chris Carey and Rob Tibbs—went to work treating the throngs of Gulu villagers who had heard they were coming to help. In all, 600 Ugandans lined up outside the building. Some sat on the ground, while others nabbed the few available folding chairs. Most had walked many miles for the chance to see a doctor, in some cases for the first time in their lives.

This would not be a one-time service. The Pros for Africa organization would go on to stock the now-public clinic with critical medicines, staff it on a daily basis, and hire a fulltime, roving physician to rotate to various cities throughout Uganda.

But the PFA trip was not all about work. It was about connecting, one person at a time, with neighbors from the other side of the world. Whitten had seen on his first visit to St. Monica's how much the female students feared men, especially those they had never met. Even by American standards, the PFA football players were enormous, giants with big hands and feet and the brute strength of animals. How could these traumatized girls ever feel comfortable around them?

To Sister Rosemary's surprise, the athletes did just what they did back home: They used their charisma, humor and warmth to win over their fans.

Wearing khakis and a white, long-sleeved Pros for Africa t-shirt, sunglasses dangling from his collar, Williams addressed dozens of girls standing in front of a row of simple bleachers on the school grounds.

"This is a game that we played in California when I was a youngster," he announced. They still play it. It's called 'Simon Says.'

"So if I say 'Simon Says raise your right hand,' everybody has to raise their right hand." Williams demonstrated by raising his right hand. He then practiced a few more examples before starting the game.

"Okay, everybody put your hands up," he instructed. Most of the girls kept their hands at their sides, but a few burst into laughter when they realized they had goofed.

Williams chuckled. "Okay, are you guys ready? Are you ready?"

"Yes," said the girls, some of whom spoke English. Now they were focusing hard on Williams' directions.

"Simon Says, 'Stand on one foot, either one you want.'" The girls did as they were told, imitating the stance of flamingos.

"All right, put your foot down." A few of the students tapped the ground before realizing their mistake. Giggling, they good-naturedly took their seats on the bleachers.

Soon, only two girls were left standing.

"All right, all right. Come closer together. Closer together." Both obeyed Williams before realizing they had been tricked. Laughing hysterically, they fell to the ground before getting back up and making their way to their seats. The girls, who had smiled so little in recent years, were grinning from ear to ear with their new friends from America. Sister Rosemary watched in disbelief, pleased to see such a miracle unfold right before her eyes.

Knowing how revered these athletes were in their home country, Sister Rosemary marveled at their down-to-earth attitude. There was Adrian Peterson, carrying a smiling child on his back and playing soccer with the girls. Over there was Mark Clayton dancing with a group of students. And the kids couldn't stop laughing at Tommie Harris when he made funny faces. She could hardly keep from laughing herself. When it was time to play soccer and volleyball, Sister Rosemary was right there in the middle of things. She even tried her hand at American football with the NFL players, shocking the athletes by catching their hard-thrown passes.

But deep down, after the laughter subsided, the lights dimmed and the "Pros" went to bed, knowing their wonderful trip was about to end, they realized they were only making a drop of difference in an ocean of need. They were just four athletes, four doctors, three lawyers, four water well engineers, and a handful of others. The needs of the girls, who had endured so much agony at the hands of Kony and his rebels, dwarfed the small but sincere efforts of the volunteers from Pros for Africa. The visitors knew they would have to do more. They would have to inspire other professionals to join the team.

Headed home, Whitten watched from the airplane window as the Ugandan landscape grew smaller and smaller and eventually disappeared below the clouds. He knew he needed to grow the organization into a sustainable effort that would support Sister Rosemary's girls, and hopefully others in need, for years to come. He also knew that it was critical for the world to remember what Kony did to these innocent children. If the world forgot, history might someday repeat itself. These young women and children must be remembered. They must be given a chance to rebuild, recover and lead a safe, peaceful life.

The next year, eleven professional athletes, most of them recruited by the original football players, provided aid in both Uganda and Rwanda. On the March 2012 trip, forty-six volunteers, including New York Jets wide receiver Santonio Holmes and free safety Quentin Carter of the Denver Broncos, descended on Gulu, where they helped build a new playground with swing sets, a sliding board and colorful tire "mountains" for the children at St. Monica's. Other big-name football players joined the Pros for Africa team, offering hands-on assistance: Vernon Davis, tight end with the San Francisco 49ers; Vontae Davis, cornerback for the Indianapolis Colts and, before that, the Miami Dolphins; Green Bay Packers wide receiver Greg Jennings; Larry Fitzgerald, wide receiver for the Arizona Cardinals; Gerald McCoy, defensive tackle with the Tampa Bay Buccaneers; Stockar McDougle, a retired offensive lineman who played with the Detroit Lions, Miami Dolphins and Jacksonville Jaguars; Jerome McDougle, a former defensive end for the Philadelphia Eagles and New York Giants; Bryant McKinnie, offensive tackle for the Minnesota Vikings and, more recently, the Baltimore Ravens; and Derrick Morgan, defensive end with the Tennessee Titans.

Then in 2013, Harris and Williams led another trip to Africa with new PFA volunteers NaVorro Bowman and Tedd Ginn, Jr. of the San Francisco 49ers.

Inspired by Sister Rosemary's unfaltering dedication to those in need, in early 2013 Serge Ibaka, an Oklahoma City Thunder basketball player born in the Republic of Congo, held a fundraiser for Pros for Africa. In attendance were his high-profile teammates Kevin Durant and Russell Westbrook, who, like so many others, were immediately inspired by Sister Rosemary and her work.

More and more healthcare experts joined the PFA team. Medical student Cayci Brickman volunteered at St. Monica's for four months before starting her studies at the University of Oklahoma College of Medicine. After that, she stepped up to lead free, annual medical clinics in Uganda and, along with her fellow OU students, raised money to send Ugandan undergraduates to the Gulu University School of Medicine. The team of OU medical school students quickly became a regular fixture at the school.

Dr. Daniel O'Donoghue, an advisor and professor at OU College of Medicine, began to visit Gulu on a regular basis to implement training for Ugandan healthcare workers, free of charge, and later taught at the Gulu university.

At the same time, numerous medical students from Oklahoma State University also volunteered to conduct no-fee clinics in Gulu each year. The students formed a student club called Pros for Africa Club, led by their faculty advisor, Dr. Kayse Shrum, the President of the OSU Center for Health Sciences and Dean of the College of Osteopathic Medicine, along with volunteer Nurses and Doctors. These hard working volunteers have saved countless lives.

One undergraduate student from OSU, Alyssa Peterson, followed in Sister Rosemary's footsteps and delivered many African babies before graduating from college. She went on to volunteer in South Africa as well.

Students from the University of Oklahoma Law School were so moved by a speech Sister Rosemary gave that they formed a student organization and began to visit St. Monica's to address legal injustices. Led by student Nazareth Haysbert, Law School students regularly traveled to Uganda to address and improve legal issues in a country where the rights of women and children have historically been lacking.

Wanting to get involved too, a group of OU engineering students went to Gulu to build eco-toilets and find ways to purify the primitive water system.

Pros for Africa not only provided direct help to Sister Rosemary and her girls; through its celebrity status it was able to network with other organizations and get them involved. One of the most significant partners was the Starkey Hearing Foundation, founded in 1984 by Bill and Tani Austin to tackle the problem of hearing loss around the world and deliver more than one million free hearing aids to the less fortunate. In Uganda, and much of Africa, people often contract malaria, a mosquito-borne infectious disease that can cause fever and headache, even coma and death. Unfortunately, some medications used to treat it also cause hearing loss. The Starkey Hearing Foundation, with help from the Pros for Africa volunteer athletes, held several hearing aid missions at Sister Rosemary's schools in Gulu and Atiak.

In 2012, the Starkey Foundation honored Sister Rosemary for her humanitarian work at its twelfth annual "So The World May Hear" gala in St. Paul, Minnesota—an event that drew dozens of celebrities and high-profile supporters, from President Bill Clinton and former Eagles singer Glenn Frey to comedians Steve Martin, Robin Williams and Billy Crystal. There, Sister Rosemary was introduced to the audience by actor Forest Whitaker, who after falling in love with the people of Uganda during the filming of the 2006 movie *The Last King of Scotland*, for which he earned a "Best Actor" Oscar for his portrayal of the infamous Idi Amin, began supporting Hope North, a Ugandan school for boys not far from St. Monica's. Founded by Okello Sam, who as a boy had been forced to serve in Joseph Kony's army, Hope North helps educate and heal the spirits of former male abductees in much the same way as Sister Rosemary's school for young women.

When Watson finally finished the documentary, three years after he recorded the first Pros for Africa trip, Forest Whitaker agreed to narrate it. With the debut of *Sewing Hope: The Life of Sister Rosemary Nyirumbe*, her story would come to life on the big screen.

As the years passed, Whitten continued to dream bigger and bigger dreams for Pros for Africa. Volunteers like executive director Bill Horn jumped on board and expanded Whitten's dreams for supporting Sister Rosemary. *Who knows?* Horn thought. *One day maybe there will be supporters in every NFL and NBA city.* It could easily happen if others followed the example set by Serge Ibaka and Tommie Harris, who had held their own fundraisers to benefit the organization.

The Pros for Africa volunteers still had a long way to go to achieve the impossible. But first, Sister Rosemary's girls in Gulu, Atiak and Torit must be cared for.

CHAPTER FOURTEEN

SISTERS UNITED

Young ladies proudly displaying the pop tab purses they made

Word of Sister Rosemary's success with the formerly abducted girls was spreading, not just in Uganda, but across the globe. Her uncanny ability to inspire people from all walks of life had motivated movie stars and pro athletes, doctors and lawyers, young students and veteran teachers, political leaders and CEOs, even JAIA (Just As I Am), an Oklahoma City musical group featuring singer-songwriter duet Lisa

Davis and Lynda Knox, who wrote a moving song about Sister Rosemary called "Touched by a Rose." In 2007, the American television news network, CNN, honored her with a Heroes Award, triggering a flurry of donations and inquiries. She had become a highly sought-after speaker on the topics of women's rights and the empowerment of women.

Increasingly, as awareness of Joseph Kony's evil acts grew worldwide, she was asked to tell her story and describe the consequences of war to humanitarian groups, school audiences and the press. Who better for the media to interview than Sister Rosemary, who was now helping several young mothers raise their illegitimate children—Kony's children—at her school?

In Scotland, she gave talks to raise money for the work of the Scottish Catholic International Aid Fund in Haiti, South Sudan and other countries. In the United States, she proudly spoke about how well her girls were doing in their vocational classes and urged audience members to visit St. Monica's. Sadly, even though Kony was no longer in northern Uganda, many people were still afraid to visit Sister Rosemary's country, which hurt its already-floundering economy and the chance for women to find work there.

"If you really want to know what is happening in northern Uganda, what we're dealing with in the aftermath of the LRA war, come to Africa and see for yourself," she urged. "I'm asking for your presence. Come work with us. Step out of your comfort zone. Take a risk."

During a break at an international women's conference in Hawaii, where Sister Rosemary and four other female speakers were giving their presentations, she struck up a conversation with the advocate sitting at the table next to her.

"I've been to the West Nile and I've seen what your people have been through," said the woman, who was from the Philippines. "But your land is very fertile, very green. You grow wonderful coffee there!"

As the two ladies chatted about the aromatic crop and shared their experiences from years of helping disadvantaged women, Sister Rosemary couldn't help but notice the small stack of purses in front of her new friend's plate.

"Those are so beautiful. What are they made of?"

"Soda pop tabs," the woman answered. "We crochet them together and sell them to raise money. This purse would sell for many American dollars."

Sister Rosemary's eyes grew large when she heard the amount.

"Here, you can have one," the woman said, handing the nun a small silver clutch. Then she removed her bracelet, also made of aluminum tabs, and placed it in Rosemary's hand.

"But I have no money to pay for these," Sister Rosemary protested.

"Please take them," the woman said. "This is my gift to you as payment for your advice about growing coffee. You can teach the women at your school how to make them."

Back in her hotel room, Sister Rosemary peered through her eyeglasses and carefully studied the bracelet and purse. The girls at St. Monica's were already making necklaces, bracelets and rosaries by rolling colorful magazine pages into tiny cylinders, gluing the "beads" tight as cocoons and applying a shiny, protective varnish. It had only taken the clever nun a few minutes to learn how to do it, and she had quickly taught her students. But a purse? That was much more complicated. And she had no instructions to go by.

Well, I like a good challenge, she thought, laughing. *Why not?*

Sister Rosemary left the women's conference and flew to Oklahoma, headquarters for Pros for Africa, before returning to Uganda.

"Rachelle, look at this," she said, pulling the clutch from her suitcase at the Whittens' house. Opening the purse, she traced her fingers across the smooth lining. Then she pried a few of the pop can tabs away from the thread and studied the stitches. "Do you think I could make these?"

Rachelle laughed. "Sister Rosemary, you can do anything you set your mind to. I have no doubt about that."

"Well, I did learn how to crochet when I was ten, and all I had to work with was sticks," the nun said. "How much harder could this be?"

"I think we can find you a more suitable crochet hook," Rachelle said, grinning.

That night, the two women experimented with a few pop tabs and some string. Unlike the horizontal rows in her Filipino friend's purse, Sister Rosemary's came out vertical. Disappointed, she was trying to figure out how to copy the sample when she suddenly realized that her makeshift pattern was actually more closely-knit, more durable than the original.

It would make a stronger handbag! The young women at St. Monica's could definitely help support themselves with a project like this.

But Sister Rosemary's delight soon turned to puzzlement. "Where will I get enough pop tabs? Where will I get the yarn?"

Rachelle simply grinned. "I think I can help with that part."

Back in Gulu, Rosemary was anxious to see if the girls could imitate her design, so she assembled a group to test their reactions. As usual, one girl stood out.

Abducted when she was thirteen, Naomi had been held captive in the bush for a year and a half before she managed to escape. Trained as a soldier for the Lord's Resistance Army, she was often commanded to attack and loot villages throughout northern Uganda. Life was quiet during the day when the rebels hid in the forest, fearing they might be discovered, but when dusk fell they would send the abductees to town to commit their prescribed atrocities. If the child soldiers refused to do what they were told, they risked a brutal punishment, perhaps even death. It was not uncommon for the guerillas to force Naomi and the other prisoners to run seven or eight kilometers without stopping, especially if government soldiers were believed to be in the area.

The teenager frequently thought about ways to escape but knew the consequences far too well. Once, she had received a command to kill one of the other girls from her village who had tried to break free. When Naomi hesitated, a boy in the group carried out the order. It sickened her to know that she might someday suffer the same fate.

But fate was on her side. One of the rebel commanders had lived in the same village as Naomi and was related to her father, and he took pity on her. "I've seen how children are treated here and I don't want to see you suffer any more," he told her. "You go, and I will stay here. Even if it means I die, let me take you and guide you home."

Months later, Naomi learned that the man who helped her escape had been killed by his comrades. She wasn't sure how he died.

It took a while for her to grow accustomed to life in the village again. She married and had two children, but her husband beat her and failed to care for his family. Like many Ugandan men, he had little respect for a wife who had spent time in the bush, even against her will. After living with her brother for a short time, a church authority arranged for Naomi to go to St. Monica's and finish her education.

She had not been attending school very long when Sister Rosemary approached her about making the purses. Naomi's first clumsy attempt didn't turn out so well. Sometimes the yarn unraveled, or the bag began to take on an odd shape, but she kept trying. Days later, Naomi held up her first success: a beautiful clutch made of rows of shiny pop tabs neatly bound together by silky yarn, ready to be lined with soft fabric. Despite the merchandising potential, to Sister Rosemary the proud smile on Naomi's face was worth more than a truckload of shillings.

None of the other girls in the group finished their purses, but Naomi completed another one without any thought of reward other than a word of praise from Sister Rosemary.

"Here," the nun said when the girl produced the second, neatly stitched handbag. "Here is your payment."

Naomi could hardly believe what she was seeing. There, in her outstretched hand, was a small stack of Ugandan banknotes.

"Yes, I am paying you for your work," Sister Rosemary said. "You did a fine job. And I will keep paying you if you keep making them, and making them well."

Naomi didn't know whether to hug Sister Rosemary or cry. Now she would be able to send money home to her mother and children. She would no longer be a burden to her family.

When word spread that Naomi had earned cash for making purses, the other girls eagerly stepped up to earn theirs.

Every day after their classes ended, a group of students gathered under one of the shade trees around a simple wooden table or sat cross-legged on a bamboo mat on the ground. Motivated by the chance to make money—something they had few opportunities to do in this poor farming town—they eagerly learned how to weave the pop tabs together using nylon yarn in a rainbow of colors: purple, red, and black; gold, royal blue and lime; white, orange and taupe. While some students crocheted, others used pliers to twist metal rings to attach to the handles, measured for pockets to accommodate cell phones, or hand-stitched linings with heavy-duty sewing needles. Sister Rosemary personally inspected each finished purse to check for flaws.

If a girl hesitated or doubted her own ability to make the handbags, the motherly nun took a "tough love" approach. "Can you speak?" she asked, her hands on her hips. "Can you work? Can you make use of your hands? Can you listen to instructions?"

Sister Rosemary began selling their wares for a meager sum at the town market and to guests who visited St. Monica's. Within weeks, she had sold more than 500 bags on behalf of the girls. Eventually, the purses commanded more money, mostly from visitors to Gulu. In the United States, she knew, their creations would bring even more.

So in 2012, Sister Rosemary and Rachelle Whitten established Sisters United LLC, a for-profit business that would serve as a vehicle for selling the bags. Thanks to Sister Rosemary's friendship with one of its employees, Tim Popp, the Anheuser-Busch facility in Oklahoma City donated thousands of pop tabs in silver, green and blue, and big-hearted volunteers across the state collected buckets of recycled soft drink tabs. Rachelle bought the crochet hooks, pliers, fabric, yarn and metallic connector rings for the handles—so many, in fact, that she and Sister Rosemary often drew attention at stores as they unloaded their carts and piled the supplies high on the checkout counter. The startled clerks had never seen such long receipts.

Inside each limited-edition purse, the Sisters United logo depicted the continent of Africa, a mother and her child, and the words "Handmade By St. Monica's Girls' School, Gulu, Uganda." All of the net proceeds went directly to Sister Rosemary's school account, which then paid the young artisans.

The operation was far from simple, and crafting even one pop tab purse by hand was incredibly time-consuming and difficult. It generally took a student an entire week to painstakingly hand-craft a large bag, something that wouldn't be economically feasible in America. In addition, the pop tabs from Anheuser Busch came in sleeves of thousands and had to be manually removed from the aluminum lids. Making the work even more tedious was the fact that the tabs also had to be washed in the United States due to the shortage of precious clean water in Uganda. So Rachelle and her team of generous volunteers, some young, some old, but all motivated by their love for Sister Rosemary and her girls, held "pop-off parties," sitting for hours and pulling thousands of tabs. Other volunteers stopped by to pick up huge bags of sleeves, remove the tabs at home in their spare time, and later return them to Rachelle.

At one pop-off party held in Rachelle's guesthouse, which she now dubbed "the second home of Sister Rosemary," the cheerful nun found herself fighting back tears. Here were a dozen women, from diverse backgrounds, in a country on the other side of the world, prying off thousands of pop tabs to send to her girls in Uganda. As they worked, their conversation flowing and laughter filling the air, the women began to bond as sisters. Their unconditional love and closeness to one another filled Sister Rosemary's heart with hope for the future of her girls.

She had witnessed a similar phenomenon in Gulu when the students gathered to make purses. As they sewed, the former kidnap victims smiled and laughed, filled with hope and at peace, growing closer to each other, all because they'd been given a handful of "trash" to transform into lovely, elegant purses. This project was truly amazing, Sister Rosemary thought, with a symmetry she'd never expected. It was a wonderful thing to behold.

Rachelle had observed the same thing, but from a different point of view. Living in a fast-paced country—the richest in the world—Rachelle couldn't help but notice that many Americans seemed unhappier and less fulfilled than the girls in Uganda, who owned very little. She also noticed that when the American volunteers stepped forward to help Sister Rosemary's girls, they seemed more content and satisfied with their own lives. Why couldn't people in the United States see that the way to true happiness is in serving those who are less fortunate? Maybe this little purse project would inspire more Americans to help someone else.

By forming a small army of women to drastically reduce the time involved in disassembling the pop tabs from the sleeves, Sisters United had solved a major problem. Now they faced a new one. How would they get the tabs and other purse-making materials to Uganda, where Sister Rosemary's girls anxiously waited, ready to work? After pondering this obstacle long and hard, Rachelle eventually came up with a solution of sorts: The airlines would allow her to carry up to nine bags (for an additional fee, of course) each time she flew to Uganda!

Rachelle and a half-dozen volunteer friends caused quite a stir the first time they arrived at the Will Rogers World Airport in Oklahoma City, toting fifty-four extra travel bags. When the puzzled security employees opened the old, beat-up suitcases, they made an unusual discovery: tens of thousands of gleaming aluminum pop tabs.

On Rachelle's next trip to Africa, airline staff members knew what to expect. They soon grew to recognize Sister Rosemary, Rachelle and her band of weary travelers. "Here come the Sisters United girls again!" they often said, grinning in amazement.

The same process had to be carried out in reverse to get the bags back into the states. This time they were filled to the brim with beautiful purses, all uniquely handmade by the girls at St. Monica's.

Each major sale was cause for a celebration—and a payday in Gulu. Accounting for each item and logging the numbers on a white ledger pad, Sister Rosemary sat at the front of a classroom at St. Monica's and called each girl by name. One by one, the girls rose, giggling, from their stadium-style seats to collect their share of the wealth.

"Now I expect you to save some of this so you'll have funds to start your own businesses when you leave here," she told them matter-of-factly. "You need to save part of every sale you make. That is part of the deal."

"Thank you, Sister. Thank you, thank you," the young women repeated, still amazed at their own good fortune.

As with any smart enterprise, the company offered a variety of products. The signature tote, called "The Rosemary," was made with more than 1,700 pop tabs. "The Monica," a smaller shoulder bag named for the patron saint of motherhood, was born when, in response to a shortage of aluminum tabs,

Sister Rosemary divided the supply in half so that no one who wanted to be involved in the purse-making project would be left out. "The Teresa" crossbody bag paid tribute to India's most famous nun. Other styles included "The Eden," with its crocheted flower pattern; "The Eternity," a small, circular bag; and "The Destiny," a backpack featuring 2,000 tabs. Because they were made by hand, with no assembly line processes or equipment, no two were exactly alike.

Despite the difficulties of the cumbersome, inefficient system of popping tabs from donated sleeves and flying them to Uganda, with Rachelle personally purchasing all of the thread, lining materials, and additional sewing machines and equipment, both Rachelle and Sister Rosemary, who had become like real sisters, knew this was only a start. A small step, but a start nonetheless. One day, they hoped, a single donor, or more than one, would deliver the pop tabs directly to the school, along with the critical thread and other components. Always positive, Sister Rosemary felt confident such a benefactor would be able and willing to shoulder this burden. Hopefully it would be soon.

In the meantime, a new and unexpected market was building for the Sisters United purses. At a sold-out fundraiser at the trendy Devon Boathouse in Oklahoma City, hundreds of women lined up to purchase the bags. And when Sister Rosemary was honored for her humanitarian work at the Starkey Hearing Foundation gala in 2012, actress Maria Bello startled the crowd when she ran to the stage to offer $5,000 for one of the haute couture purses.

Despite the glamorous reception, what pleased Sister Rosemary most was knowing that the project was making a difference in the lives of her girls. The sale of a single "Rosemary" bag enabled a young woman to pay her school fees, living expenses and meals for one year. Just one "Destiny" backpack purchase covered all annual necessities, plus a few "luxuries" like sugar and toiletries, for a mother and her child.

Jeanette, a former Night Commuter who had at one time fled to St. Monica's for safety at night and later graduated from the tailoring course there, was so good at quality control that the Sisters asked her to supervise stages of the project. She and Naomi, the first girl to master the art of purse making, were hired in the production section of the tailoring center and were able to make a living for their families.

But none of the girls was more grateful for her newfound source of income than Faye, a soft-spoken young woman with a pretty face, tightly woven dreadlocks, and long, slender fingers with which she deftly hooked her crochet needle into the yarn as skillfully as if she had done it all her life.

Unlike most of the students at St. Monica's, Faye managed to avoid abduction by the Lord's Resistance Army. She grew up in the Soroti district of eastern Uganda, in a town dotted with ornate Hindu temples and Muslim mosques that fell into disrepair after President Amin systematically drove the Asians out of his country in the 1970s. A gigantic rock—a volcanic plug, a natural phenomenon caused by the hardening of magma in a vent of an active volcano—towered at the edge of the village market. Adventurous souls often climbed to the top to drink in the magnificent panoramic view of the nearby lakes and mountains.

Such a feat was impossible for Faye.

Crippled by polio at the age of four, her legs were so badly twisted and weak, her feet so misshapen, that walking was painful and she often stumbled and fell. To take just one step, she had to pick up her leg and set it back down on her toes, which curled under like fleshy claws. Sleeping was, at best, uncomfortable. To shift from one side to the other in bed, she first had to struggle to sit up, then position herself just right before carefully turning over.

Many times, her family heard that the rebels were coming and hurriedly grabbed a few belongings on their way out the door. Because Faye couldn't walk very fast, and running was out of the question, her parents took turns hoisting her behind one of them on a bicycle or carrying her on their backs.

Twice, compassion for their grown daughter almost got them killed when her disability slowed them down and the rebels nearly caught up. A few times, her parents hid her instead of taking her with them, but risked being kidnapped when they sneaked back to check on her. Even after the LRA war began to subside in northern Uganda, the danger still lurked.

Faye grew more and more anxious. "What am I going to do? My mother and father are going to lose their lives because of me. I can't let that happen."

Sneaking out of the house so her parents wouldn't try to stop her, she begged rides to get to Mbale some seventy miles to the east. A handful of Sisters of the Sacred Heart of Jesus lived in a small convent there.

"Can you please give me some work and let me stay here?" she asked the nuns as she watched them survey her deformities. "I can work hard. I can do it."

But the Sisters had no jobs to offer, and no place to keep her. The place was full, they said, and they had no money.

Not wanting to burden her parents and too proud to go home, Faye remembered her friends who lived not far away. She moved in with them temporarily, waking early each morning to go into town to earn money by cleaning groundnuts. Wiping the soil from the legumes, which were destined for stew or nut butter, was no easy task. To earn a mere 2,000 Ugandan shillings—about eighty cents in American dollars—Faye had to sort and clean 100 kilograms, or 220 pounds, of groundnuts with her bare hands. Cleaning the sackful of nuts took all day and, if she failed to finish, she was paid nothing for her labor.

Despite the hardship and the fact that the nuns had turned her away, she continued to pray every morning at the Catholic church before work. The Sisters took notice and were impressed by her diligence and strong religious faith.

"Faye, come here," one of the nuns said as the young woman prepared to leave for the market. "Until now, we have turned down your request. It is time for you to come and help us. We will make a place for you."

Before long, they had promoted Faye from plate washer to cook and were paying her 20,000 Ugandan shillings a month. A year later, when the money ran out and the nuns could no longer afford to compensate her for her time, they called their colleague Sister Rosemary in Gulu. She would not have the heart to say no.

Faye was thirty-three years old when she arrived at Saint Monica Girls' Tailoring Centre, exhausted from the daylong bus ride and dragging her small suitcase behind her. Anxious that she was so far behind in school—she didn't even know how to write and had completed only a few of the classes "required" for admission—she wondered how in the world she would make it in this big, sprawling place.

Faye had heard much about Sister Rosemary, who was away on business in the United States. "Where is the Sister who is headmistress here?" she asked the other students.

"Oh no, she's not just the headmistress. She's the director of the school," they said. "She runs the place."

"What does she look like?" Sister Rosemary must be quite old, Faye assumed.

"No, she's not that old," her new friends assured. "She's kind, and very funny. You'll see."

When Sister Rosemary returned from her trip, Faye caught a glimpse of her in the hallway. The nun looked much younger than she had imagined, especially when she was smiling. Now Faye was even more curious to meet this mystery woman.

The following day, Faye was recruited into a group of young women who were learning to craft handbags with nylon thread and pop tabs. She had never crocheted in her life, and she was nervous. But Sister Rosemary was patient with her instructions and generous with her compliments as she taught the girls how to loosely wrap the yarn around their fingers and hook it through the loops.

"Faye, you are holding the needle like a man. You are supposed to hold it like this," Sister Rosemary teased, adjusting the girl's fingers. Faye giggled, and the other students laughed out loud. "If you do this, you can go faster."

After the lesson, Faye thanked Sister Rosemary for the chance to learn something new. Unlike most people, who openly stared at Faye's legs, the jovial nun seemed to look past the disability.

It took Faye four days to learn how to crochet the purses without dropping a stitch or accidentally varying the size of the rows. She loved the feeling of making something with her own hands, and she loved the result. Her favorite style was The Teresa, the small crossbody bag crafted from 520 aluminum tabs.

In the summer, when some of the girls took a holiday to visit their relatives back home, Faye stayed. She had no money to get to Soroti and her parents couldn't afford to visit her at the school. One day a nun pulled Faye aside. "We need you to come to the house," she said, pointing to the building where she and the other Sisters lived. "We want you to help us with something."

Sister Rosemary was waiting in the sitting room. "Faye, it is so good to see you! How are you doing?"

"I'm doing well. Thank you for asking." Faye smiled but inside she was worried she'd done something wrong.

"I wanted to talk to you about something. I see that you have trouble walking, especially with our many stairs, and that you fall down all the time."

"Yes, Sister."

"Well, I don't like it and I'm going to do something about it."

Faye hung her head in shame. Perhaps Sister Rosemary was just like the others after all, focusing too much on her disfigured legs.

"I am going to take you to the hospital in Kampala," Sister Rosemary continued. "It's painful for me to see you moving like this, and I think we can fix it. I don't want you hurting any more."

Faye was touched, but baffled. What would happen at the hospital? How much would it hurt? And how would she pay for it?

"But I've done nothing to deserve this," she said quietly.

"Yes, Faye, you deserve it. We are going to do this."

Back in her room, Faye prayed, *Father, I am a sinner, your servant. Give me the strength to go through with this and to heal, because I don't want to let Sister Rosemary down. She is like one of the kind people in the Bible who laid the paralyzed before Jesus. She is an angel whom you have sent to help me. Lord, help me to do as she asks.*

Armed with funding from Pros for Africa and Sister Rosemary's longtime confidante, Father Luigi, the two women set out on the dangerous road to Kampala. Political demonstrations, which sometimes turned violent with riots in the capital city and the surrounding areas, had once again made traveling difficult.

Faye was uneasy, concerned not for her own safety but for that of Sister Rosemary. *What if something happens to her? It will be my fault, just like it was my fault that my parents were almost killed by the LRA soldiers. I don't think I could live with myself if someone harmed her.*

But Sister Rosemary would have none of such negative thinking. After making their way to Kampala, past all the roadblocks and security checks, they met with the surgeon. Faye was astounded when she heard how much the operation was going to cost, and that didn't include the special crutches and fittings she would need afterward.

"Don't worry about the money," the nun soothed. "What I want is for you to walk better. That is what would make me happy. The money—that is no problem. I trust in the Divine Providence. And always, when I trust in the Divine Providence, I receive what I need. God gives me the money to help people."

Faye healed quickly from her surgery and was soon able to climb the school steps with her new braces, without lifting each leg with her hands. Now that her once-uneven limbs were the same length, she could start to gain the muscle tone she had never had.

It wasn't long before she began making purses again, determined to repay Sister Rosemary for her kindness. Like many of her classmates, she was unaware of the scope and intent of the project and thought she was just passing time with Sister Rosemary. And, like the other girls, she was shocked when Sister Rosemary called them together to pay them for their work.

"What?" she exclaimed, staring at the wad of bills in her hand. "This can't be possible!"

"It is possible," Sister Rosemary assured her. "Believe in your work and believe in yourself."

Faye saved part of the money, sent part of it home to her family to pay for her sisters' school fees, and bought herself a few things at the open market. In her mind, Sister Rosemary was a miracle worker, restoring her physical body and giving her a newfound sense of hope. Each time Faye tutored one of the new girls, showing them how to crochet the purses, she mindfully exercised the same patience Sister Rose had shown *her* when she was first starting.

As she had many times, Sister Rosemary set her sights high. Not satisfied with knowing her students were the only ones who knew how to craft the potentially life-sustaining purses, she taught the other Sisters at St. Monica's, then set out to educate the nuns and novices in the neighboring convents, including her own religious training ground in Moyo. She was pleased to find that some were experienced tailors. Some already knew how to knit, crochet and embroider, so they learned quickly.

"You are the future of this mission," she told them. "If I am no longer at St. Monica's, if I die, you can continue the work that is going on there. If we are really dedicated to helping the needy, we must make sure we teach them how to sustain themselves. We are here to promote women within our society, and this is one way we can do that."

Sister Rosemary was now dreaming bigger than ever. Her goal: to empower as many women as possible in northern Uganda, to coax out their inner beauty and help them discover their worth.

Many people, she knew, would spot a pop tab in the dirt and consider it trash. Her girls were a lot like those tabs—overlooked, discarded, treated with disdain. Many of the young women had been defiled in captivity and were thought of as nothing more than garbage by the men they now chose to love and the suspicious families with whom they had reunited after escaping from the bush. But here, retrieved from the rubbish, polished and woven together by their common bond, they had become beautiful treasures to be admired and adored.

CHAPTER FIFTEEN

WAR OF THE HEART

One of the houses made from recycled bottles at St. Monica Girls' School

The Lord's Resistance Army began vacating northern Uganda in 2006, at the start of peace talks between the Ugandan government and the LRA in Juba, Sudan. Instead of signing the Final Peace Agreement, as he had promised to do several times, Joseph Kony moved his militant forces into the border regions of southern Sudan, the Democratic Republic of Congo and the Central African Republic. In 2008 the United

States government officially identified Kony as a "Specially Designated Global Terrorist," and in 2010 President Barrack Obama signed into law the LRA Disarmament and Northern Uganda Recovery Act, aimed at stopping Kony's attacks. In late 2011 President Obama sent 100 American special forces advisors to Central Africa to help scour the dense jungle for one of the world's most vicious terrorists, who was still at large.

Bit by bit, the people of northern Uganda began to recover, to rebuild their homes, replant their farms and go back to school. The LRA war was over, but the war in the heart of the formerly abducted girls was not. The emotional healing would take much, much longer.

Nevertheless, one strong-willed nun had served as a positive influence in the lives of hundreds of young women and children. Tough and tenacious, hardworking and humble, she had fought for their rights as human beings and their futures as productive members of society. By establishing an integrated daycare center, teaching the girls practical skills they could rely on long after graduation, and standing up for them when others doubted their worth, she had given them hope and a sense of belonging they had not known for quite some time.

Instead of brushing them aside, as their families and neighbors had done when they emerged from captivity, hungry for acceptance, she had taken the time to sit with them, to listen to their stories, no matter how horrific, without passing judgment. When some of them later found out they had acquired HIV/AIDS, she arranged for them to get treatment and counseling, and she even hired a few infected girls as support staff, making sure no one singled them out. She loved them all unconditionally, and they knew it, and that had made all the difference.

Her encouragement never stopped, even after the young women graduated from St. Monica's. "The past is gone. It cannot be changed. You can't take it back," she often told them. "But you can start over right now and live for today. And if you can live for today, you can live for tomorrow. Always think about hope, and walk toward that hope. It will give you the strength to be the person you are meant to be.

"Yes, you have bad memories," she acknowledged. "And your life may not be easy. But you can still make something of yourself. If your leg is crippled, you can still use your hands. If your lips are cut, you can still see. If you are pregnant, with no husband to take care of you, you can still be better than you are today. And you can actually marry a great man, even if you have been held captive by another, even if you have born his children. You do not have to settle for anything less."

In the assembly hall at St. Monica's, Sister Rosemary sometimes challenged her students to go a step farther. "Repeat with me: 'I can change the world.' Say it. You can do it."

"I can change the world," the girls said in unison, softly at first, then with more confidence. "I can change the world!"

Despite her religious vows, Sister Rosemary did not believe in standing on a pedestal, preaching to people and trying to convert them to Jesus Christ with her words. Many times, she was asked, "Sister, do you teach these girls about religion, about God?"

Sister Rosemary had her own way of doing things, and she felt no need to apologize. "No, I don't. I believe in the gospel of presence, in working with people to minister to their needs and meet them where they are. If I weren't religious, I would not be a Sister. That's why I'm here. But I believe that our lives should show who we are and what we believe. We should practice our faith rather than preach it."

She began to notice that as the girls healed from their psychological wounds, as their self-esteem rose and their hearts became lighter, they actually became more physically beautiful. The school, too, had blossomed, with a computer lab, a half-dozen sewing classrooms and new pink buildings—a house for the child mothers, a thriving clinic, a daycare center and kindergarten—next to the cream-colored ones dotting the campus when she first arrived. The windows were now open during the day, shutters thrown back to let in the light. After school, students rested on bright blue benches near thickets of pink bougainvillea, strolled the grounds with their babies on their backs, or crocheted pop tabs together to make purses to sell. They were, after years of living with fear and regret, starting to feel safe again.

Sister Rosemary was quick to point out that she could never have done it alone. The NGOs and other charitable organizations, such as Pros for Africa and Sisters United, had provided critical funding to keep the school going. And her capable staff—well, without them, she could never have reached for the stars. Sweet and soft-spoken, Rosemary's deputy director Sister Asunta handled day-to-day operations, from discipline to scheduling to academic programs. Sister Polyne ensured that the nursery and daycare were running efficiently. Sister Christine was in charge of sustainable agriculture. Another Sister Christine oversaw handicrafts, supervising production and making sure the girls had enough fabric and other materials to work with. Sister Elizabeth, a paramedic, ran the clinic. Sister Margaret served as the matron for the school, in charge of student welfare. Not everyone was cut out to work at St. Monica's, Sister Rosemary knew, so she was careful to ask the Catholic Church to send Sisters who would be a good fit. Their dependability and moral support allowed her to do what she did best: network with humanitarian organizations, secure funding, report to donors, recruit volunteers and, most importantly, be a mother and mentor to her students.

There were still plenty of challenges. Electricity remained in short supply, not just at Saint Monica Girls' Tailoring Centre, but throughout northern Uganda. Without electricity, no water could be pumped from the well, and without water the school was not a safe place for young women and children. Without computer access, some classes screeched to a halt. When the electricity *was* working, the bill was often more than the Sisters could pay.

Sister Rosemary refused to let such obstacles hinder the progress of the school that had grown from a haven for a handful of scared, withdrawn students to a bustling campus known for its skilled, capable graduates. With a financial boost from Pros for Africa, the second St. Monica's school finally opened in Atiak, a town that had suffered greatly under the regime of the LRA. The project had begun years before, when Atiak residents implored Sister Rosemary to come to their village, pick up the formerly abducted women who were living there, and take them back to St. Monica's in Gulu.

"That's a wonderful idea," she told the other Sisters, and set about packing her bags. But when she arrived, she found not a dozen, not thirty, but 150 child mothers who needed a place to live while resuming their basic education and training for new careers.

"I can only take fifty," she told the young women, her heart breaking at the thought of leaving anyone behind. "Instead of taking you all to Gulu, we are going to start a branch of St. Monica's here, in Atiak."

Sister Rosemary had no idea how she was going to keep her word, but somehow, she knew, she would. God would find a way. Sure enough, the donations appeared, paving the way for a smaller version of the main school in Gulu. It took many years to complete the primary construction, but in 2009 the second St. Monica's campus opened in Atiak with two classrooms for tailoring lessons, a multipurpose classroom, living quarters and a public clinic open at scheduled times. When the nursery and daycare were unveiled in 2012, plans were underway for catering classes and a restaurant designed to serve travelers on the highly trafficked route between northern Uganda and the country now called South Sudan.

The enterprising nun also made plans to build a third St. Monica's school in Torit, South Sudan, near the Ugandan border, and train Sudanese nuns to run it. Home to the Catholic diocese from which her own congregation was born, Torit had also endured the atrocities of the Lord's Resistance Army, leaving a number of formerly abducted girls and their children with no way to support themselves. Besieged by fighting between rebel factions and the northern Islamic government of the capital of Khartoum, the area was still unsafe, prompting some of Rosemary's advisors to urge her to abandon her plans. That, of course, didn't stop her, and she kept up her efforts to open a branch in Torit.

Sister Rosemary decided to name the school after a special Pros for Africa philanthropist named Ashley Firmin Harris, the young wife of NFL star Tommie Harris. The couple had volunteered together to help Sister Rosemary at both Gulu and Atiak. When the huskier NFL players, like her husband, toiled away at dirty, physically demanding tasks, such as digging shallow water wells with the Oklahoma non-profit group Water4, Ashley jumped right in. Sister Rosemary held a special place in her heart for Ashley and could tell she would be a lifelong supporter.

Sadly, that life ended too soon. Not long after giving birth to her second child in early 2012, Ashley suffered a sudden and catastrophic aneurism and died at the age of twenty-nine. Ashley would never see the school named in her honor, but Sister Rosemary was determined to insure that her work with Pros for Africa and St. Monica's would not be forgotten.

Construction is, however, extremely challenging in South Sudan, Africa's youngest country. Clean water is scarce. Building materials are rare. Ever the shrewd entrepreneur,

Sister Rosemary heard about a machine that turns the red clay of that region into sturdy bricks and began strategizing on how to buy two of them, one for Gulu and one for South Sudan. While brick-making is difficult work usually done by men, Sister Rosemary knew that her girls, many of whom were once reluctant warriors kidnapped by Kony's soldiers and living in the jungle against their will, were up to the task of running the machine. The brick-making equipment could also generate much-needed income for the schools and ease Sister Rosemary's worries about how to feed the children and keep the doors open at St. Monica's. For now, though, the technology was financially out of reach, so Sister Rosemary must find another way to build her next structure. If creative thinking could turn pop tabs into purses, why couldn't she turn trash into a house?

One day when Sister Rosemary drove past a landfill, she spotted thousands of plastic pop bottles piled high. *Those ought to be good for something*, she noted. Wasting no time, she directed her students to gather the empty, discarded bottles and bring them to St. Monica's. Then she logged onto her computer and surfed the Internet for a way to use them. What she found made her smile. *Perfect*, she thought. *An answer to many prayers.*

Soon, the girls were filling the bottles with sand. "Brick" by brick, they assembled unbreakable, fortress-like houses, stacking the sturdy bottles toward the sky, bundling them with nylon string to hold them steady, and cementing them together with wet dirt and clay while leaving ample spaces for windows and doors. By the time they had finished, the young women had built an entire house strong enough to withstand powerful winds and swift floods.

Sifting through some old files one day in her office, Sister Rosemary noticed a long-forgotten document that brought a smile to her face.

She began to read aloud: "Training in only tailoring for three years does not provide enough opportunity for these girls and women who otherwise want other courses for life skills and problems. For this reason, the center embarked on practical dressmaking and basic cookery for one year. This course is offered especially to formerly abducted women. It also has become a process of continuous rehabilitation for these girls."

The report was ten years old. Sister Rosemary had written it one year after arriving at the lifeless, "grossly underutilized" Saint Monica Girls' Tailoring Centre.

She glanced at the shelf near her desk. On it lay a used artillery shell from the fall of Idi Amin in 1979, a daily reminder of how long her country had been sabotaged by power-hungry dictators and war lords. The most recent, Joseph Kony, had inflicted his own brand of cruelty on the people of northern Uganda and forever scarred the girls at her school. In the face of such trauma, another school director might have merely offered a safe, quiet place for the former abductees to hide from a world that now shunned them. But Sister Rose was no ordinary director. And this was no ordinary school.

In her first year at St. Monica's, she had begun preparing the students for life beyond the sheltering walls of the compound, arming them with job skills to support their children, themselves and, in some cases, their relatives back home. In the decade since, she had launched a strong and respectable catering program, rented the main hall many times to raise money for the school, and offered the girls a chance to practice their newly-acquired skills by serving guests at seminars, workshops, weddings, graduations and church meetings. Her tailoring students were sewing uniforms for schools in Gulu, outlying towns in Uganda, and South Sudan. Other girls had learned to craft jewelry and pop tab purses to sell in the United States. Many had graduated and gone on to land jobs in the hospitality industry, jobs that enabled them to eat every day rather than go hungry or rely on relatives who had treated them with disdain and mistrust since their return from the bush.

Encouraged by the words in the ten-year-old report, Sister Rosemary read the document in its entirety. Despite all the naysayers and detours, frustrations and challenges, her outlandish ideas had blossomed into real, proven programs that had made a real difference. It had been an incredible journey, for her and the girls, and for everyone whose lives they had touched.

But Sister Rosemary's work was far from over. There were many more girls to nurture, more children to cuddle, more programs to launch. It would be like building a house, one brick at a time, for a growing family that never seemed to have enough room. She would keep dreaming big and reaching high. She would keep reaching out to the women and children of Uganda. And she would continue to live by the mantra she had often repeated to skeptics, to her colleagues, to the world, "We are here to heal the wound in any way we can."

EPILOGUE

BY SISTER ROSEMARY NYIRUMBE

I have lost count of how many women and children we have served at St. Monica's since I came here in 2001. Many of the girls keep in touch long after graduation, mentoring the new students, bringing their children back to the school to visit, and even stopping by to check on me. When word got out that I broke my leg and had to wear a cast for six weeks, they brought me gifts and stayed with me for hours, helping me in and out of my chair while I adjusted to my new crutches. When I told them they were being too nice, they said, "Sister, you cared for us. Now it's time for us to care for you." I received a lot of love and care from the students, former and present. Rosemary Kojoki, one of the children I cared for from the time she was six months old, looked after me day and night with much love and attention.

I have learned so, so much from these girls. They are beautiful, resilient and determined to overcome the past. They have taught me what it means to have courage in the face of grave danger. They have reminded me just how strong women can be.

Imagine a girl who was forced to kill her own little sister. Imagine the guilt, the grief, the bitterness she must feel toward her captors. Imagine what a difficult task it is to move on from the nightmare she has been living for years.

The heartbreaking stories never stop. Just when I think I've heard everything the child mothers could possibly tell me, someone shares a memory that is more horrifying than anything I have heard before. Yes, they will always bear the scars—emotional, psychological, and physical—of what they have been through. The scars will remain but they do not have to be so painful, and they do not have to hurt forever. It is not our job to erase them. It is our job to help heal the deep wounds in their hearts.

Many of the girls I've worked with over the years have forgiven their abductors, but not themselves. They still agonize over the brutal acts they were forced to commit and the choices they made in a desperate effort to save their own lives. No matter how accomplished they are in their careers, or what wonderful mothers they have become, they simply cannot let go of the guilt that haunts them. I tell these women, "There is no sin which cannot be forgiven. In fact, you are *already* forgiven. God the Father sent his Son to die for all of us, to set us all free." It is the only time I preach to them.

A girl who is unable to forgive herself leads a suspicious life, wary that everyone around her is staring at her, talking about her, plotting against her. Once she starts to forgive herself, even a little, you can see a big difference. She stands up straighter, smiles more and even becomes more physically beautiful. Her shoulders are no longer tense and tight from the weight of her emotional burdens, and she begins to open up, trust others, and make new friends.

Forgiveness is a long journey. It is not about letting go of the painful memories in a minute, an hour, a day. It is about learning to see yourself and another person in a different light. It is about walking with someone day after day, learning who they really are—their weaknesses, their strengths, their humanity. It is about unconditional love. It is about letting go over time.

There are many girls out there who still carry deep pain in their hearts. We will always be here for them, to lift them up and restore their dignity through love, care and acceptance. I want the women and children of northern Uganda to have the best education possible. I want them to have peace of mind and joy in their hearts. I want them to leave our school with the ability to forgive others as God has forgiven *them*, to accept others as *they* were accepted.

My hope is that St. Monica's will continue to expand and become an even better place after I'm gone. We have many more women and children to serve. The faster we move, the better. There is no time to waste.

The older I get, the more my dreams grow, and the clearer my visions get. I have learned that if you keep your dreams to yourself, they won't work. If you share them with other people, good things happen. If you dream big things, big things happen.

I will never stop dreaming big.

AFTERWORD

BY REGGIE WHITTEN,
CO-FOUNDER, PROS FOR AFRICA

It's been over eleven years since I lost my son Brandon and almost that long since Sister Rosemary Nyirumbe came into my life. Oddly enough, it seems a lifetime ago and, at the same time, almost like it was yesterday.

Africa was good for me because I learned that what I went through with losing my son, although terrible, was far less tragic than what these innocent children of Uganda and South Sudan went through. Now, any time I am having a bad day or get depressed, I just think back to the suffering of these children.

I often think back to the day Sister Rosemary cut the ribbon at the Brandon Whitten Hall at the new school that Pros for Africa started in Atiak, Uganda. I could tell that my friends who accompanied me were moved, some to tears. But no one was more emotional that day than Sister Rosemary. I watched her suffering. Tears streamed down her face and she could barely talk when she gave her speech. She even had a little plaque made to commemorate the day.

I wondered, *How is it that Sister Rosemary hurts so badly over the loss of this young man that she had never met? Why did she feel such pain over this untimely death that occurred on the other side of the world?*

Then I realized why. Sister Rosemary is like a sponge; she has this uncanny ability to drain the pain away from others. For at that very moment, while I was contemplating her tears over the loss of my son, I realized that I was hurting less than usual, while she was suffering vicariously for me.

And in that moment, I learned that in this one small way, I knew a little about how these young captives, who had escaped slavery and torture, must feel when they are around Sister Rosemary. Just as she did with me, Sister Rosemary helps drain the pain away from these young ladies. I have seen that strange phenomenon many times now, and it's always the same. Hundreds and hundreds of young women have come through the doors of her schools, all of them with enormous pain and agony. But when they encounter Sister Rosemary, they find a sense of peace, they grow, they regain some of their dignity.

But this doesn't come without a price to Sister Rosemary. With her unique ability to empathize with her students, she takes their pain onto her shoulders. She wears it well, but it is a heavy burden nonetheless.

I can truly say that in all my travels across several continents, I have never met anyone like her. We live in a society where the word "hero" is perhaps used too easily. But what a hero she is!

It is remarkable that she was not killed during the terrible years of the war caused by Joseph Kony and the LRA. What would we do if LRA thugs showed up at our door and demanded the return of one of their sex slaves? Would we have the strength and courage to tell them no, when they were holding guns and machetes in their hands? Would we be brave enough to hide an escaped girl under our bed, when we knew we would be killed if they found her?

I am in awe of the work done by the amazing Mother Theresa. She was incredibly deserving of the Nobel Peace Prize. But how could Sister Rosemary be less deserving?

I know that I will never have the power or influence to see that Sister Rosemary is nominated for the Nobel Peace Prize. Indeed, Sister Rosemary wants neither accolades nor wealth. She takes her vow of poverty very seriously. But I dream of a day when she is nominated for that very award. And I knew that her story must be told from the time I first met her.

The world must never forget what happened in Uganda and South Sudan during the reign of terror by Joseph Kony. His name must live in infamy forever, alongside other such mass murderers. It is by remembering Kony's evil deeds and atrocities that we keep them from happening again. Make no mistake about it; if the world forgets these kinds of human rights violations, they will happen again. History always repeats itself, and a short memory makes it more likely to happen.

But it's not enough to remember the Hitlers, the Stalins, the Konys. We must also remember the heroes who stood up to those evil tyrants, and Sister Rosemary Nyirumbe is paramount among them.

It must also be remembered that even after the war ended, Sister Rosemary's job was far from over. Much of the danger was gone, but the job got even more difficult in some ways. Even though Kony has left Uganda, he has also left all those shattered lives behind. Who was going to pick up the pieces?

Sister Rosemary could have gone elsewhere. She didn't have to go to Gulu, or Atiak, or South Sudan. She voluntarily took on a monumental and thankless job.

It is essential that the eyes of the world remain on Uganda and South Sudan. These children of the war must never be forgotten, lest history follow in the footsteps of tyrants once again. The schools created and maintained by Sister Rosemary are building young lives that will change the world in a good way. She is raising young women up to stand on her shoulders. She is indeed as deserving of the Nobel Peace Prize as anyone who has ever earned that great honor.

But she will not hear of awards or accolades, for her work continues. Every day, it's a challenge to keep her school open and running.

I will never forget the day Sister Rosemary gave me and my oldest daughter a tour of a rural village, not far from where Alice Lakwena started the Lord's Resistance Army movement. That day, three medical students from Oklahoma State University Medical School were putting on free medical clinics for the people of northern Uganda. We stopped in a small village where a young mother had recently died, leaving behind three young children. Sister Rosemary saw that these orphans had no one to raise them. Without hesitation, she calmly told the village elders that she would be back tomorrow to take these orphans to her school. She didn't check her budget to see if she could afford it, nor did she check to see if she had room to take three more orphans. She just did it, because someone had to. It was another example of how she took the pain of others onto herself and quietly shouldered the burden.

Her story had to be told. The world had to know about Sister Rosemary. Telling this story has been a long journey undertaken by my friends and fellow volunteers at Pros for Africa, but we now have the story in book and movie form. Now we can only hope everyone gets a chance to see and hear it.

You may be asking yourself: Where will Sister Rosemary and her girls go from here? It's an excellent question. Sister Rosemary will never ask for anything, other than for everyone to visit her at one of her schools. She will welcome you with open arms. Winston Churchill famously called Uganda the "Pearl of Africa." Sister Rosemary feels the same way about her girls. She will smile that big grin of hers and proudly introduce you to her girls, for they are truly "Pearls of Africa" in her mind.

What does Sister Rosemary need? That answer is simple. The needs of the children of northern Uganda and South Sudan are nearly infinite. She needs a little bit of everything, but Sister Rosemary was raised never to beg. She will never ask for a handout, instead wanting to simply create jobs for her girls. She is the ultimate entrepreneur, but she needs the tools to establish commerce. We here in the richest country in the world can give her those tools with minimal effort if we just try.

There are two interesting things that I have learned since working in Africa: First, everyone who visits Sister Rosemary's girls is blown away. One hundred percent of her visitors are moved to the extreme and universally make statements that they will help when they return home. Sadly, life is busy for us all and fewer than half ever follow up with promises made while visiting.

The second interesting thing that I have learned is this: Since forming Pros for Africa, I have been approached by dozens of well-meaning people who make statements like, "You know what you ought to do to help Sister Rosemary? You should do this...."

Sister Rosemary and I have compared notes and we often laugh about this strange phenomenon. As they say, talk is cheap! If it's so obvious that *we* should do this, why doesn't the person who has this great idea do it? It seems that many people assume that someone else is doing the necessary heavy lifting. Unfortunately, while the folks with all these good ideas are talking, the victims of Joseph Kony's war are going without basic necessities and Sister Rosemary's school is on the verge of closing.

As John F. Kennedy famously stated, "Ask not what your country can do for you, ask what you can do for your country!"

In the same vein, Sister Rosemary and her girls desperately need for volunteers to come up with ideas *and* take action!

Pros for Africa was built on the concept that we are all professionals and can do something. Indeed, we have numerous examples of individuals, young and old, taking action. One of the most beautiful examples was six-year-old Cate, who instead of asking for her friends to bring her toys to her birthday party for her own enjoyment, she requested that they bring toys to send to Sister Rosemary's schools! Because of this one little girl, the daycare in Gulu now has a lot of colorful toys.

Or Laura, the yoga instructor, who didn't have much, but brought dozens of Danskin outfits and who instructed these former abductees in the fine art of yoga and laughter.

And there was the case of the software designer and entrepreneur Noah Roberts, who took a leave of absence from his CEO position to serve Pros for Africa for a year. Pros for Africa volunteers come in all sizes and shapes, in all walks of life, proving that anyone can help the less fortunate in Africa! All you have to do is care!

We have seen so many volunteers spring into action, from the aspiring movie maker Derek Watson, to the many incredible doctors and medical students holding volunteer medical clinics, to the lawyers and engineers plying their trades, to artists painting beautiful murals on the formerly bland walls, or the friends back in the states holding "pop-off parties."

Taking action is the key. We all can do something. But not all of us can go to Uganda. If you can't go, you can help Sister Rosemary collect pop tabs, or you can donate. You don't have to be wealthy to help. I won't forget the young student, who after hearing Sister Rosemary speak at his school, pulled out his only five dollars from his pocket, and pressed it into Sister Rosemary's hands to send to the school. Everyone can do something!

Perhaps the most amazing irony is that while we are helping Sister Rosemary and her girls, we are the ones who stand to gain the most. While we are building structures and providing clean water and keeping the lights on at the school, it is actually we who are helped. Despite the fact that we live in the richest country in the world, so many of us have holes in our hearts. We are the ones who benefit the most from helping these formerly abducted girls. Going to Africa saved my life and it has brought meaning to the lives of hundreds of the Pros for Africa and Sisters United volunteers. It can do the same for you.

As I write this last page of the incredible story of the life of my dear friend Sister Rosemary Nyirumbe, I think of the last time I saw her. She was smiling with that incredible mischievous grin of hers.

"I will not stop dreaming," she said, and she smiled again. She is still smiling today. If you don't believe it, come see for yourself. The doors to her schools are always open. But don't plan to sit still too long. She will put you to work! And you will sleep well that night.

ABOUT THE AUTHORS

Reggie Whitten is a graduate of the University of Oklahoma ('77) and its law school ('80). He practices law fulltime in Oklahoma City with the firm of Whitten Burrage and is a Fellow of the American College of Trial Lawyers, which limits its members to the top one percent of a state's attorneys.

In his spare time, Whitten visits schools throughout Oklahoma to recount the story of his eldest son's death from an addiction to prescription drugs. It was this tragedy that led Whitten to meet Sister Rosemary Nyirumbe and begin his philanthropic work. The co-founder of two organizations, Pros for Africa and FATE (Fighting Addiction Through Education), he previously co-authored a book about his son's addiction, *What's Your Fate?*, with his dear friend Jim Priest. In honor of his son Brandon, who loved dinosaurs as a child, Whitten also co-founded ExplorOlogy and co-founded Native Explorers, an educational program that seeks to inspire young people to get involved in science. To date, more than 53,000 kids have completed the program.

Whitten was inducted into the Oklahoma Hall of Fame in 2013 and currently lives in Edmond, Oklahoma.

Nancy Henderson is an award-winning author who often writes about people who are making a difference through their work. Her first book, *Able! How One Company's Extraordinary Workforce Changed the Way We Look at Disability Today* (BenBella Books, updated hardback edition, 2008) tells the story of a factory owner whose practice of hiring employees with physical and mental disabilities catapulted his rug manufacturing company to international success.

Henderson has published hundreds of articles in *Parade, The New York Times, Smithsonian* and other periodicals. She is a member of the prestigious American Society of Journalists and Authors and lives in Chattanooga, Tennessee.